Doing College Right

A Guide to Student Success

JOE O'SHEA

TEACHERS COLLEGE PRESS

TEACHERS COLLEGE | COLUMBIA UNIVERSITY

NEW YORK AND LONDON

Published by Teachers College Press,® 1234 Amsterdam Avenue, New York, NY 10027

Copyright © 2020 by Teachers College, Columbia University

Front cover: Photo of college student by Cookie Studio / Shutterstock.

Library of Congress Control Number: 2020944750

ISBN 978-0-8077-6482-4 (paper)
ISBN 978-0-8077-6483-1 (hardcover)
ISBN 978-0-8077-7930-9 (ebook)

Printed on acid-free paper

Manufactured in the United States of America

Doing College Right

This book is dedicated to Karen Laughlin (1949–2020), a mentor, colleague, and tireless advocate for student success.

Contents

PART III: DEVELOPING FULLY

Acknowledgments

This book would not have been possible without the generous support and feedback I received from numerous friends, colleagues, and students, especially Elliana Cooper, who provided many thoughtful contributions and edits. I am particularly grateful to Florida State University and Sally McRorie for enabling me to write this book, as well as to the many thousands of students and families with whom I have worked over the years. Finally, I thank my family for their incredible patience and encouragement.

Getting In Is Not Enough

Lucas sits down at his computer in the evening, waiting for colleges to send out their admissions decisions. He's eager to hear from an in-state school, where he can already picture himself attending. His family gathers around him. They're excited too, because Lucas will be the first one in the family to go to college. Lucas anxiously refreshes the webpage until a decision finally appears. It's a yes! He and his loved ones are ecstatic. Everyone is joyous, hugging each other and jumping up and down in celebration. But Lucas and his loved ones have no idea that he is one of the many students whom the higher education system will fail. He will drop out of college in his sophomore year.

Lucas is not alone. Across the United States, each year about one million students (around 40%) will leave higher education without a degree, adding to the 36 million U.S. adults in 2019 who had some college education but no degree (Shapiro et al., 2019). These students often find themselves in a bind. They don't have the college degree that allows them to access many higher-paying jobs, but they are saddled with student debt (Kirp, 2019b) that can significantly damage their credit score if they default on payments."

Especially disheartening is that those who do not graduate are disproportionately students from underserved communities, like Lucas. Higher education's failure to elevate graduation rates for much of its student population undermines its promise to lift students and their families toward economic and civic prosperity. Sadly, some colleges can perpetuate inequality, creating obstacles in what is supposed to be a path of opportunity. Over the years, working with thousands of students and their families, I've seen firsthand the enormous capabilities students have and how colleges and the higher education system can fail to realize that potential. But I've also seen how students, armed with the right information and attending a college designed to foster student success, can grow to the fullest.

Students and their families want more than just to graduate—students want to leave college having taken full advantage of their time in higher education, launching successfully into the next stage of their lives. Getting a good start has never been more important. Technological developments prompt rapid changes in the economy and the labor market, and the skills students develop in college can transfer across jobs and throughout careers, helping insulate them from changing economic conditions.

It's no surprise, then, that the wage gap between those with a college degree and those without has increased over the years, and college graduates earn upwards of a million dollars more over a lifetime (Carnevale et al., 2015). Research has also found that college graduates tend to be happier, healthier, and more engaged parents and voters than those without college degrees (Oreopoulos & Salvanes, 2011). Furthermore, college can cultivate the foundational characteristics that help students live in diverse communities, underpinning citizenship and public life.

Given the positive effects college can have on our lives, it's no wonder that getting in has become high stakes for many. In 2019, the FBI revealed that for the past decade, wealthy parents had bribed and deceived officials at prominent colleges around the United States to gain acceptance for their child in a college admissions scheme dubbed "Operation Varsity Blues." In total, the parents spent more than $25 million to manufacture test scores, fabricate students' athletic profiles, and bribe coaches.

As this college admissions scandal highlighted, the allure of and competition for entrance to the most selective colleges has reached new heights. Getting into the most "elite," "best," or most popular college can be all-consuming, shaping much of a high school student's life.

In response to the scandal, pundits across the country proclaimed how broken and toxic our college admissions process is and that students and parents should stop focusing on the most selective schools and chasing prestige (Robbins, 2019). Others declared that students should stop trying to mold themselves to fit the top colleges. Instead, they claimed, students need to find the school that "fits" them in order to find success (Klunder, 2019). And many argued that it doesn't matter where you go to college, that you can be successful anywhere you go (*Chicago Tribune* Staff, 2019). In other words, it's the student who defines their trajectory, not the college.

The intense process of getting into college makes it hard for students to see past the admissions office and to really assess which view on student success is true. They often ask themselves important questions: Which college should I attend? And what should I do during college to thrive? Is success possible anywhere, and what does it even mean to succeed? For most students, answering these questions is hard—often, they don't know enough about what actually makes a difference in determining success to make the best choices. Even more, the programming and support offered by colleges has become so complex that it is hard to even understand how everything fits together to help students. Students now have a dizzying number of ways and options to engage in higher education.

Consider this example: Samantha has just been accepted to college. She has a choice between two seemingly similar institutions. Both public, both in the same state, both of which have high rankings on different lists and offer many activities, sports, and majors—but students are nearly twice as likely to graduate in 4 years from one college than from the other. Why? And where should she go?

THE CHANGING COLLEGE LANDSCAPE

In past decades, the classic story during new student orientation was that a college leader would stand up and tell students, "Look to your right. Look to your left. One of the three of you won't be here by the end of the year." Many were proud of that claim, arguing that it meant the college was upholding rigor and that only the strongest would make it through.

Colleges have come a long way. With rising tuition rates and demands for accountability, efficiency, and performance, student success has become a primary focus for higher education. Institutions now profess that they want all of their students to succeed, even declaring that they have an obligation to do everything possible to help each student they admit to graduate. Colleges have implemented countless programs and initiatives in hopes that their students, regardless of their background, will graduate and launch into fulfilling careers. Research supports these efforts. As a national study found: "Students' perception of the degree to which the institution was supportive of their academic, personal, and social needs was the most powerful predictor . . . of increased academic competence" (Reason et al., 2006).

Higher education professionals now know much more than they once did about how students learn and develop, and how they can design colleges to promote the full educational growth of students.

What has become clear is just how much the many variables of the college experience actually affect students' success: where you live during college; how you engage, both in the classroom and beyond; which courses you take and the type of instruction in those courses; the extent of mental health, advising, and career planning support; the levels and kinds of financial aid; and participation in experiential and applied learning. In short, student success depends on the ways colleges engage, challenge, and support their students.

Many students looking for guidance on college encounter an abundance of contradictory advice and myths that surround college, from friends, online forums, colleges, advertisements, and so on. These sources tell students about the quality of institutions, what and how they should study to have a good career, what organizations they should join, where they should live, and what the "college experience" entails. Students are inundated with information and material. But even with all this input, college can still seem like a labyrinth, full of complex procedures, unfamiliar vocabularies, mysterious rules, and nebulous pathways. Colleges have particular ways of being that can make them seem like a foreign world to students. Consider this bewildering passage from a college's former graduation requirements:

> In order to uphold the policy that students may take a 1000 to 3000-level Scholarship in Practice course to meet one of their General Education Electives, there is one minor exception to the policy limiting the number of Social Sciences, History, or Natural Sciences that can count to meet the elective. Specifically, if students meet three hours of the General Education Elective requirement with a Social Sciences, History, or Natural Sciences course and also take a Scholarship in Practice course that is approved for that same General Education area, the course will count as a General Education Elective due to the Scholarship in Practice designation. (Florida State University Registrar, 2019, p. 89)

All of this can leave us with uncertainty along the path to and through higher education. How exactly does one complete all the requirements? How does a student apply for financial aid? What is undergraduate research? How does one build a competitive resume for graduate schools or employment?

The underlying challenge is that much of the college advice students receive places too much responsibility on the student in student success. A common claim is that a student doesn't do well in college because the student has deficits, not because something was poorly designed or run at the institution. People are too quick to think a student didn't do well because they couldn't understand the material, or they didn't ask for help, or they had poor time management skills, or they lacked motivation, or they didn't want to engage on campus. Unfortunately, emphasizing the student as the determinant in student success perpetuates a paradigm that success is solely determined by the students.

The truth is that higher education institutions themselves can be designed (or not!) to facilitate student success. In fact, colleges that have very similar student bodies can still have graduation rates that vary by 20% (Kirp, 2019b). Many postsecondary institutions still deploy insufficient strategies to promote student growth and address differences in students. This results in a very leaky pipeline to and through postsecondary education. Fortunately, colleges have begun to realize that they too have deficiencies, ushering in a shift away from a largely student-deficit paradigm to one that includes an institution-deficit paradigm in which colleges recognize how they are not meeting the diverse needs of their students.

As we will explore in this book, both the college and the student matter in creating student success. Where you attend college matters because colleges are different from one another—and the college you attend very much influences what you do in higher education. Institutions can help students fully develop their potential, shape their aspirations, engage academically and socially, and navigate through their higher education journey and beyond.

Some colleges are much better than others at doing this. They intentionally design their institution to support student success—by curating opportunities, support, and experiences for their students, particularly for students who are historically underrepresented in higher education, so that success is more widespread.

A first-year student in a science course, for instance, could have her confidence and identity derailed by a poorly designed and ineffectively taught course, with a professor who appears to the students as condescending and not interested in helping students succeed. When she asks a question in class, the professor responds, "You don't already know that?" which inhibits her from seeking help and feeling empowered. What this first-year student doesn't know is that the evaluations of this professor's teaching have been negative for years, and the university hasn't intervened to support improving his teaching. This student's abilities and identity, however, could have been ignited by effective teaching, mentorship, and pathways that provide support and encouragement to ask questions, explore, and grow.

Despite vast differences in colleges' abilities to promote students' growth, it's easy to be attracted to colleges for reasons less connected to student success, like social activities, a friend who attends the college, or slick recruiting. Some students may be especially drawn to what seems to be the cheapest or the closest college. While this is attractive in the short term, it can be costly, particularly if the college is not sufficiently designed to support student success and therefore reduces the likelihood of graduating in a timely fashion.

That said, colleges can only do so much—engagement and success also depend on the student and their willingness to connect, grow, and learn. Students need to find a college that will inspire and foster their growth *and* they need to be equipped with the perspectives to discern what is available and how they should allocate their time for success.

HOW TO USE THIS BOOK

This book is designed to serve as a guide to help you navigate higher education and give you the perspective to maximize educational growth. It harnesses the latest research on how students develop and showcases award-winning programs from colleges around the United States that make a difference in students' lives. This book illustrates students' experiences by telling the stories of fictionalized college students based on persons and experiences I have witnessed. Drawing on this combination of research and narratives, the book provides a framework for evaluating colleges and making decisions about higher education, and it prioritizes students and their success in doing so. Because so much of the college journey can be complicated, we'll take a measured approach to evaluating each component. Throughout the book, I recommend different questions to ask of colleges. A good starting point in asking these and other questions is the college's admissions office, since staff there can help locate information and connect you with their appropriate colleagues at the institution as needed.

There is no precise formula for success applicable to every student; there is no magic bullet or one-size-fits-all approach across the full higher education landscape—there are different contexts and student populations with varying needs and wants. Students arrive at colleges with a host of complexities and life challenges that become part of their college experiences. As we will explore more in the book, the diversity of students and higher education institutions necessitates a holistic definition of student success, one that focuses on the full development of students across their many domains.

Consider this book to be an expert on your side as you explore colleges, make decisions, and transition through the higher education system. Using this book will help you find the best college for yourself or someone else in your life. While there are many types of colleges, all of which contribute to a diverse landscape of higher education, this book will be most helpful for those seeking to attend a 4-year college. Even if you don't have a choice in which college to attend, this book can help you prioritize how to spend your time in college. It will help you see beyond all the flashy materials and sales brochures, understand what the evidence really says about student success, and determine what to do before and during college to thrive.

THE BOOK'S STRUCTURE

The book is structured to help you make decisions along the journey through college.

In Part I, Prioritizing Student Success (Chapters 1 and 2), we orient ourselves to the college experience and the decisions we make along the way. We start with a survey of the higher education landscape and then move to some foundational questions about college choice, prompting you to think about what student success should be in higher education. We also examine ideas and myths about which kinds of colleges yield the best results for students, asking questions like, "What are the different kinds of colleges?" and "What are rankings and how should we understand them?"

In Part II, Excelling Academically (Chapters 3 and 4), we tackle the core of higher education: the classroom and curriculum. We examine the decisions students must make about what and how to study, as well as the most effective forms of teaching and student support, including mentorship and advising.

In Part III, Developing Fully (Chapters 5, 6, and 7), we look beyond the classroom to experiential and applied learning, like internships, study abroad, and other transformative, career-building activities. We also look to the research on students' extracurricular life, such as the social networks students are involved in and ways students engage on campus and in student clubs. We end this part examining personal wellness, exploring the national data on well-being—including mental health, safety, and physical wellness—and seek to identify what colleges offer and the decisions students can make to promote healthy living.

In Part IV, Funding and Launching from College (Chapters 8 and 9), we examine costs and financial aid, and look beyond college graduation toward what students should do to successfully prepare for employment or graduate school.

In the Concluding Thoughts, we'll wrap up everything and revisit some lessons learned surrounding student success and the roles colleges can play in fostering it.

While the journey to and through college can seem overwhelming, it's important to remember that there are pathways to success for *every* student. All students can succeed in higher education with the right perspectives and an environment that engages, challenges, and supports them. This book will help you find those places and thrive when you get there.

Part I

PRIORITIZING STUDENT SUCCESS

CHAPTER 1

Changing Expectations
The Student Success Movement

Jim is on an official college tour with his daughter Sarah. He's especially excited for her to see this college because it's the same one that he attended. Standing on the campus, he's struck by a wave of nostalgia. The architecture of the buildings hasn't changed, still the same old red bricks he remembers. There are students playing Frisbee and lying out on the grass studying, the same as he had done. But as the tour continues, Jim notices more and more differences. When the tour observes a classroom, Jim sees that the class is lively and animated. Instead of standing at a podium for an hour, this professor breaks the class into small groups and moves around the classroom. This is a far cry from the lectures that Jim remembers. When they pass by a chemistry lab, the tour guide points out a group of first-year students working alongside a professor in a research lab. From what Jim recalls, only graduate students had that kind of opportunity.

As Jim and Sarah move across campus, Jim reads the flyers advertising student events, for organizations like the Haitian American Student Organization, LGBTQ+ Student Association, and Hispanic Student Union. The student body that Jim recollects didn't have any of these organizations; most of the people in his classes looked like him, White, and came from similar economic backgrounds. At the end of the tour, Jim and Sarah pass a building that he doesn't recognize. When Jim peeks inside, he sees students in business professional clothing, sitting down with staff to review resumes or talk about job opportunities. The tour guide explains that this is the new Career Center, designed to give students the resources and empowerment to graduate from college and enter into the workforce or graduate education. As Jim listened to the tour guide, he reflected on his idea of student success. Back when he attended college, he considered students to be successful when they made it to graduation. But now seeing all the different opportunities afforded to students, it appeared to him that there might be a more expansive view of student success and all that it could entail.

Jim's story points at how the nature of many colleges has changed in the 30 years since he was an undergraduate. What college looks like, who attends, and the opportunities available within higher education have shifted over the decades. As these changes have occured, so have changes in how students, families, and colleges think about student success. In this chapter we'll discuss what student success is and how to identify colleges that prioritize it.

WHAT IS STUDENT SUCCESS?

Student success is a term often heard in education, but what does it actually mean? And who says whether you are successful or not? The answer depends on who you ask and has changed over time.

For much of the history of higher education, college was an exclusive opportunity for a limited number of people. Colleges were mostly homogenous, largely serving males, particularly White males, from affluent families who had similar levels of preparation before arriving at college. Adding a layer of intellectual polish for this narrow population was seen as producing student success. But after World War II, there was an increasing desire to educate a much broader part of the population. The nation sought to expand higher education and created the GI Bill to fund college and graduate school for millions of returning veterans. As the economy continued to evolve and globalize, more people saw the need for a college education in order to have a good job and advance in a career. Colleges saw large increases in the number of students from diverse backgrounds who were seeking an education and being encouraged to enter colleges. Propelling this growth, many public colleges received additional government funding for every student they enrolled. Most existing colleges expanded, while new ones were established to address the needs of the growing population.

Despite these shifts, student enrollment in higher education did not fully reflect the diversity of the society around it. There were still far fewer people of minority backgrounds enrolled than their presence in the population would suggest, owing to social and educational inequalities seen throughout primary and secondary education. Deprived of access to higher education, underrepresented populations' social and economic mobility was limited—having a college education increases a person's lifetime earnings and enriches personal, civic, and professional well-being. Even as the U.S. population became more diverse, the diversity wasn't reflected in who actually enrolls in college, which is disproportionally students who are White. People called on colleges for a renewed focus on access: Who is being admitted to, and actually attending, college?

Broadening access to higher education was thus an initial focus of the student success movement. Colleges were assessed in the media and by policymakers for the diversity of their student bodies. Were they, for instance, enrolling more students of color or students from low-income families? Institutions launched new scholarships and recruitment efforts to broaden their student body. Newer colleges, such as those in California and Texas, enrolled increasingly diverse student bodies, in large part because of the growing population bases where they were located. As a result of these efforts, colleges were celebrated for diversifying their student bodies, while some critics claimed that colleges were lowering their standards to increase diversity. Others maintained, and continue to do so, that colleges had not done nearly enough to diversify their student bodies.

As higher education continued to evolve and colleges admitted more diverse student populations, pressure mounted on colleges to examine whether their students were actually *successful* after they started college. Did the students start but drop out or fail out? Throughout the 1990s and 2000s, the focus broadened to the retention of students in U.S. higher education. Traditionally, most students who drop out of college do so sometime between their first and second years; thus, higher education developed new retention goals for their students. Colleges sought to retain, or keep, higher percentages of their students to their second year, setting goals of retaining, for example, 80% or more of their students. Still, many students continue to leave college after the first year. Of the 3.5 million students in the United States who enrolled in a college for the first time in the fall of 2017, only 74% returned the next year, meaning over a quarter did not (National Student Clearinghouse Research Center, 2019b). And the retention rates are not distributed evenly. There are gaps along racial and ethnic lines: For students who are White, the rate was 78%, but 70% for students who are Hispanic and 66% for students who are Black.

Scholars and researchers began in earnest studying what makes students persist in higher education. From the 1970s through the 1990s, Vincent Tinto created and refined one of the first and most foundational models to explain college student dropout and retention, which is still widely referenced today (Mayhew et al., 2016).

Based on the research, Tinto argued that retention and persistence was determined by a combination of student characteristics and a student's integration and involvement in the college. Other research began to support this, finding that student engagement, both academically and socially, was critical to success, and without it, students can become isolated and leave higher education. As this student engagement–focused paradigm became more prominent among higher education leaders, colleges launched numerous first-year student engagement programs, aiming to increase involvement and student connection and belonging at the college.

It became clear that many institutions had been originally designed to serve a smaller and less diverse student body and were unready for students with different needs, expectations, and levels of college preparation. Colleges launched countless programs and services to keep students engaged, challenged, and supported on campus, resulting in elevated retention rates at many institutions. Still, many critics of these efforts blamed students for leaving higher education, asserting that the students who left were unprepared or couldn't handle the challenges and pressures of college. College leaders replied that they weren't reducing rigor or watering down the college experience to increase retention rates. They were removing arbitrary and unnecessary barriers and providing the support students needed to thrive. They also maintained that the quality of the education was not sacrificed— in many cases, removing arbitrary barriers to learning and integrating new approaches to teaching increased all students' education growth.

The student success movement then broadened its focus to include the completion of college. The new questions became: Are students graduating? How many years is it taking them to reach graduation? And are students of various backgrounds finishing at the same rate? For instance, do students from lower-income families graduate at the same rates as their wealthy peers?

According to one of the largest national student surveys in the United States, about 90% of first-year college students believe they will graduate from college in 4 years or less (Pryor, 2012). Unfortunately, only about 40% of students graduate with their bachelor's degree in 4 years (National Center for Education Statistics, 2017a). Only about 60% will graduate within 6 years, with ranges from below 30% to over 90% across individual colleges in the United States (McFarland et al., 2019). Colleges, governments, and national associations joined forces in efforts to lift graduation rates for college students, resulting in incremental increases.

The student success movement has also expanded to examine with new intensity what happens to students *after* they graduate from college. In some sense, people have always looked to what happens to students after they graduate as an indication of the quality of the college and to make predictions for themselves if they were to attend the institution. It's not uncommon for colleges to promote the celebrities, politicians, CEOs, and award-winning artists who have gone to their college. But colleges are going beyond just touting famous alumni and are looking at this matter with more data than ever before. Did their graduates get jobs or enroll in further education? What salary did they make? How much debt did graduates have, and were they able to pay back student loans? Were students from lower income backgrounds able to move into higher income brackets after they graduated?

The postgraduation outcomes, derived from the questions above, are targets for many campuses to improve, with policymakers, governing boards, and others measuring what happens to students after they graduate. Many colleges have set goals and launched initiatives to help their graduates enter the next phase of their lives. Meanwhile, critics argue that colleges do not have any control over what happens to students after graduation, or that it's not the role of the college to prepare students for employment and beyond (Fish, 2012). Nevertheless, the positive results of reforms and programming make it clear that colleges have the potential to do much more to help students develop skills and prepare for life after graduation.

WHAT SHOULD DEFINE STUDENT SUCCESS?

The measures of student success outlined above, such as who accesses, stays in, and graduates from colleges, as well as how they do after they graduate, are helpful in evaluating options and measuring colleges. They give students quick insights into the likelihood of graduating from a college and doing well there (and after). These metrics also offer policymakers ways to hold the performance of colleges accountable to taxpayers' money.

However, these simplified outcome measures of student success are alone insufficient to fully capture the growth that can happen to students in higher education. After all, success varies for every student, and most students want more than to just graduate or to get any job afterwards. They want their talents to be realized, to develop into the person they can become, and to find a meaningful role in the world where they contribute.

This raises a fundamental question: Is the college really providing an educational experience of high quality, and are the students developing to their full potential? Developing a student's full potential is something that can easily be overlooked, and is difficult to measure. It's quite possible, for instance, that a gifted student could pass through a college, receive high grades, and graduate, but not really be challenged enough to develop their full potential.

The quantitative measures policymakers use to measure student success don't capture whether colleges really have achieved full educational growth among their students. Other, qualitative dimensions of student success include the ability to think critically and ethically, work in teams, communicate, problem-solve, and more. We need to make sure students graduate and can launch into their next stage after graduation, but also that they have developed foundational skills and characteristics that will transcend their careers and personal lives. Undergraduate Joe Guidubaldi (2020) shared how his understanding of student success grew throughout his college experience:

> I initially viewed school as a place to take classes and get good grades. . . . As I have progressed as a student, I have realized that there is an opportunity for growth in every activity, and that the accumulation of these activities and growth are what really form students into their present selves. (para 5)

Student success, therefore, includes more than just making it to graduation or getting a job; student success includes the full development of students across professional, intellectual, civic, and personal domains. This more holistic conception will guide the book.

MAKING SURE A COLLEGE PRIORITIZES STUDENT SUCCESS

Having a sense of the college's understanding of—and commitment to—student success is foundational to evaluating a college. In the following chapters, we'll examine how you can evaluate and measure a college in more detail, including its approaches, strategies, and rankings, as well as other quantitative measures. But first, how can you determine a college's definition of student success, and whether they are committed to it? We can look for signals as to the college's vision, values, and culture with respect to its concept of student success.

First, assess vision: Does the college have a vision for student success? Is the college's vision for what they want for their undergraduates aligned with what you want? A college may have articulated a vision for student success, or at least produced some language gesturing toward what they want for their students and graduates. In doing so, they could speak of student success in a myriad of ways. A college could indicate in a mission statement or admissions publications, for instance, that they regard a student as successful just for graduating. Success could also be expressed as a goal of eliminating disparities in graduation rates between segments of their student body.

Others may focus on the employment outcomes of their graduates, or on the social mobility they propel. One college might say, "95% of our students are employed within six months of graduation" or "We have a high rate of students going to PhD programs after they graduate." A college may also be more specific and express the kind of graduate they aim to produce, or the skills or qualities they are striving to develop in students. For instance, Agnes Scott College's SUMMIT effort purports to reinvent "a liberal arts education for the 21st century by preparing every student to be an effective change agent in a global society" (Agnes Scott College, 2015, p. 1). Similarly, the University of California–San Diego promotes specific, career-ready competencies for their graduates (University of California–San Diego, n.d.).

Another common vision of student success is derived from *who* colleges enroll. Some colleges talk about success in the context of enrolling students from strong academic backgrounds in high school, perhaps touting that they "enroll the best students from across the nation." Likewise, you should consider whether a college considers the entire student body in its visioning. Some colleges invest heavily in the success of first-year students, but fail to take the same approach throughout the rest of their college experience. Similarly, a college might only provide strong support for students of a certain background, leaving nontraditional students struggling to find success.

Second, assess values: Are the college's values orientated toward student success? Does the college openly discuss student success and its desire for students to thrive? Does it deeply value high-quality teaching? How and where is that communicated, and what priority does it take? You may see, for instance, in admissions materials or on websites something to the effect of "student success is our top priority," or they may signal that they care about success for all students, using words like "inclusive excellence" and promoting values, work, and success to this end. For many years, President Freeman Harobski of the University of Maryland–Baltimore County has been celebrated for his student success–first drive for his college, anchoring decisions on the impacts on student success and transforming the college to maximize success for its diverse student population (Bowie, 2018). This language valuing student success might also be evident in a college's mission or vision statement, which can typically be found with a quick internet search.

You may instead get signals that the college principally concerns itself with something other than undergraduates and their well-being, or is not student-centered. If a college heavily emphasizes its research activity, graduate education, or its desire to earn more revenue, while neglecting to mention markers of student success, it may be communicating where its true priorities lie. In fact, as leadership expert Adrianna Kezar (2018) argues, as colleges have changed and expanded, doing more things, many colleges have slowly moved beyond teaching and student learning as a primary mission and are no longer structured effectively to support this mission.

A college should measure student success in specific, tangible ways, setting clear, comprehensive goals that are assessed regularly. After all, if a college is serious about creating student success, they will want to have metrics to ensure they are meeting them. George Mason University's 2014–2024 strategic plan, for instance, has specific goals for several dimensions of student success, including regular assessment of graduation rates and students' career outcomes, as well as students' views on how the college helped them grow personally and professionally (George Mason University, 2017)

Third, assess culture: Do you see a commitment to students throughout faculty, staff, and even other students? Is there a palpable culture of student success—an *every-student-matters culture*? In other words, is the success of every student seen as integral to the overall success of the college? It's easy for a college to minimize a problem related to student success, saying that it only affects a small portion of their student population. But for those students, the difficulties that they face may feel insurmountable and seriously affect their college experience, finances, and postgraduation outcomes.

Do the students say they feel that the college truly cares about them, has their backs, and wants them to succeed? During students' undergraduate journeys, they will want to be surrounded by people who are welcoming and responsive to their questions and needs. Not only should the culture be inclusive, it should also be widespread. If only the faculty or staff members in a particular department are quick to respond to students' needs, those in other departments may struggle. As David Kirp advises, college presidents should "get all hands on deck, developing a campus culture where everyone, from the president to the custodian, feels a sense of responsibility for students' success and students understand that they are valued members of a caring community" (Kirp, 2019a).

However, as we will discuss more in this book, it's possible (and often easy) for a college to speak about student success, but not actually deliver an educational environment that facilitates it or has good results. Material from public-facing sources, such as advertisements for the college, may not present a clear and accurate sense of a college's culture. After all, almost any college can claim they care about their students and want them to be successful without following through. In future chapters, we'll examine sources that can help you get a fuller view of the college's student success focus.

In short, the college should make student success a priority, regularly reviewing the whole student experience to ensure its students are engaged, challenged, and supported to grow to their full potential. We'll look at the ways we can measure student success at colleges in the next chapter.

THREE GUIDING QUESTIONS TO ASK ABOUT A COLLEGE'S PRIORITIZATION OF STUDENT SUCCESS

1. What is the college's definition of student success?
2. To what extent is there an every-student-matters culture?
3. To what extent does the college continuously try to improve its efforts in student success?

Table 1.1. A Rubric for Evaluating a College's Prioritization of Student Success

Level	Indicators
Excellent	College has well-articulated and widely understood vision and goals for student success that aim to develop all students to their full potential, both during and beyond college; college is guided by an every-student-matters culture; student success is a top priority, guiding operational decisions and the college's strategic efforts.
Good	College has clear goals and high expectations for student success; focus is on graduation rates with nominal mention of postgraduation outcomes; strong culture of caring for students with coordination of efforts to advance student success, though other priorities in the college often trump it.
Average	College has clear goals to increase quantitative measures of student success; an every-student-matters culture is present in some departments, but largely absent in others; complacency toward average retention rates or lack of student development exists.
Fair	College has a desire to promote student success, with limited goals and measures; a weak every-student-matters culture is present; college doesn't allocate appropriate resources or prioritize student success, with general acceptance of large parts of the population not graduating.
Poor	College has a weakly articulated vision for student success; explicit and implicit focus is placed elsewhere with little strategic effort to lift student success; priority is on student enrollment rather than on completion.

CHAPTER 2

Seeing Beyond the Rankings

Maria has been accepted to a well-known college in her state. When she goes over to her friends' houses, she often takes a few minutes to say hi to their parents. They usually ask how her senior year of high school is going and, inevitably, where she will be attending college next year. After Maria tells them, the most common response she gets is some version of, "Oh, what a good school!" Maria is excited and flattered by their praise but wonders what it actually means for her college to be "good."

Maria's story raises important questions: How should we measure a college's quality? Does the kind of college you attend really impact whether you will be successful?

In this chapter, we'll dig deeper into what this all means, and discuss some widespread ideas about student success at different kinds of colleges to help you get a better idea of whether you'll be successful at a given institution.

WHAT ARE THE DIFFERENT KINDS OF COLLEGES?

Many people approach the college choice process with biases or preferences for certain kinds of colleges. They want a college with top rankings or a large public college or a college close to them. The Carnegie Foundation for the Advancement of Teaching's classification of colleges, managed by the Indiana University School of Education, is a helpful system for illustrating differences among various types of institutions. Since colleges change and grow over time, their classifications may also change, but you can visit the Indiana University website for the full listing and updated information (carnegieclassifications.iu.edu). These institutions serve different populations and regions, and they all have a role to play.

While the issues and topics addressed throughout this book are applicable across the many kinds of colleges described below, I will use the word *college* to stand in for all colleges and universities, and my primary focus will be institutions that grant (at least) bachelor's degrees.

- **Doctorate-granting Universities:** These are colleges that award all levels of degrees, including PhD degrees and professional doctorates, such as from medical or law schools. Within this category are sub-classifications that separate universities by the amount of research activity and related factors. These include Very high research activity (R1); High research activity (R2); and Doctoral/Professional Universities (R3).
  » Institutions with an R1 designation are often the large state public universities, like the University of Michigan, the University of California–Berkeley, and the University of Oregon, and they also include many well-known private universities, like Harvard, Tulane, and Boston College. Cutting-edge research and creative (artmaking) work by faculty members occurs throughout these colleges. The undergraduate experience, thus, is influenced by this activity, and at many of the colleges undergraduates are able to participate in this research with faculty, an experience we will explore later in the book.
- **Master's Colleges and Universities:** These are colleges that have undergraduate and master's degrees but do not offer many doctoral degrees. Arkansas Tech University, Ashland University in Ohio, California State University–Long Beach, and The College of New Jersey are all examples.
- **Baccalaureate Colleges:** These are colleges that primarily offer undergraduate degrees. Thus, the population of these colleges is generally undergraduate students, though a few graduate students may also attend. The focus of these colleges, then, is bachelor's-level students and their education. Colleges at this level are often private colleges with smaller student bodies; some have only a few hundred students total, making for a very intimate experience. Examples include Pomona College in California, William Jewell College in Missouri, and High Point University in North Carolina. Some of the smaller branch or satellite campuses of large public colleges, like Penn State University's branch campuses around Pennsylvania, also fall into this category.
- **Associates Colleges:** These are colleges that predominantly offer associate's (2-year) degrees and not bachelor's (4-year) degrees

or graduate degrees. These are often public community colleges, like Nashville State Community College and Bunker Hill Community College in Massachusetts. These colleges often have significant numbers of students who transfer to another college after completing their associate's degree to pursue a bachelor's degree. This category also includes colleges that have a specific focus on preparing students for trades and specific vocations, such as manufacturing, aviation, culinary arts, and more. Examples include Atlanta Technical College in Georgia, Tidewater Community College in Virginia, and Yuba College in California.

- *Special Focus Institutions:* Colleges in this category are generally private colleges and have a narrow focus on preparing students in a single field or set of related fields, such as health professions, business, engineering, arts and design, law, and others. The colleges can offer 2-year degrees, 4-year bachelor's degrees, or even graduate degrees. Examples include the American Academy of Art in Illinois, Concorde Career College with campuses in several states, Brooklyn Law School in New York, and the Culinary Institute in Texas.
- *Tribal Colleges:* These are colleges that are part of the American Indian Higher Education Consortium. These colleges are often located on Native American reservations and offer either 2- or 4-year degrees. Examples include the Little Big Horn College in Montana, Leech Lake Tribal College in Minnesota, and Northwest Indian College in Washington.

Beyond the Carnegie classifications above, there are other ways of categorizing colleges. Historically Black Colleges and Universities (HBCUs)—such as Florida Agricultural and Mechanical University (FAMU), Howard University in Washington, D.C., and others—developed during times of segregation. Hispanic Serving Institutions are another classification of college in which at least 25% of the college's students identify as Hispanic. Examples include Florida International University in Miami and the University of Houston.

Moreover, institutions, at all levels, may emphasize a particular set of majors. Often this is seen with colleges that have large enrollments in science, technology, engineering, and mathematics (STEM). An institution with the word Technical or Polytechnic in its title, for instance, is likely to have a focus on technology-focused fields. While these sorts of colleges may offer a range of majors, the majority of students are likely in STEM fields. Because these colleges have a more targeted focus, students may have more opportunities for specialization. Understanding the majors a college offers, as well as how student enrollment varies across the different majors at a college, can be important to the student experience.

Let's look at Olivia. When she was a high school senior, she applied to three colleges: two that she was reasonably sure she would get into, and one she wanted to attend, but wasn't sure if she'd be accepted. After Olivia was accepted to all three colleges, she quickly decided that she wanted to attend the one that was the most prestigious. She wanted to be able to say that she went to such a competitive school and impress her friends and family. Olivia was interested in studying history. She knew that the college was mostly focused on the sciences, so she checked the college's website to make sure that it had a history program. Satisfied by a quick glance at the website, she committed to going to that college.

Once she began attending, though, Olivia realized that the program wasn't as robust as she'd imagined. She found that the number of faculty members in the history department was small, especially compared to other departments, which meant that there were only a handful of classes available each semester. The college often brought in guest speakers to discuss the latest developments in engineering, but she couldn't remember the last time there had been a historian guest lecturer. Most of the college's resources went toward research in the sciences, and she was left feeling somewhat unsatisfied with her decision. The history department, glossy website aside, turned out to be lackluster. The smaller range of courses meant that she rarely had the opportunity to take classes outside of American or European history, for example, because those courses just weren't offered at her college. Likewise, her extracurricular involvement was limited by the lack of clubs and student organizations focused on her academic interests. Looking back, Olivia wished she'd gone beyond the superficialities of attending a big-name college and paid closer attention to the particularities of what she wanted.

Just as Olivia shouldn't have disregarded colleges without prestige, we shouldn't categorically dismiss colleges based on a single dimension or its kind or category—it's important to examine the full range of a college's activities and offerings.

UNDERSTANDING RANKINGS

As students consider what types of colleges might be a good fit for them, a common inclination is to go first to the rankings. Rankings have increased in influence over the years, as legislatures, media outlets, boards, and others have funded, celebrated, or even punished colleges for their movement in the rankings. As Steven Bahls (2019) writes in the magazine *Trusteeship*:

> Americans love rankings, and college and university rankings are considered important measures of institutional performance. . . . Organizations that publish rankings make the argument that the rankings cut through the clutter of information about institutions of higher education and thereby provide a useful tool for students and others in comparing the relative performance of institutions. (p. 30)

The most popular list of rankings for American colleges is produced by *U.S. News & World Report* and is typically the list people reference when they provide a ranking for a college, like when they say "that's a Top 20 school," or "they are ranked in the top 100 of public universities." *U.S. News*'s list is primarily a measure of undergraduate education. As of 2021, there are several broad categories that compose their methodology. The first is Academic Reputation, which asks hundreds of college leaders around the country to rate each college's undergraduate academic quality on a scale of 1 (marginal) to 5 (distinguished). The second is Faculty Resources, which includes things like faculty salaries, class sizes, and student-to-faculty ratio. The third is Retention and Graduation Rates, which measures the percentages of students who retain and graduate from the college, including how many graduate above or below what *U.S. News & World Report* predicts will graduate from that college based on several variables about the college and the students who attend it. The fourth is Alumni Giving Rates, which measures, as a proxy for student satisfaction, the percentage of alumni who donate back to the college each year. The fifth is Expenditures, which measures how much money a college spends on education each year. The sixth is Graduate Indebtedness, which measures the average student loan debt of graduates and the proportion of graduates with debt. Finally, the seventh is Student Quality, which measures the SAT/ACT scores of each incoming first-year class, as well as the percentage of students who were in the top 10% of their high school graduating class.

The most prominent global rankings of colleges are the *QS Rankings* and the *Times Higher Education* rankings. These rankings use similar measures as the *U.S. News & World Report* rankings, but there are important differences. The *QS Rankings* leverage a large international survey of faculty members as well as employers to assess a college's reputation, as well as the impact of the research produced at the college. Both the *QS Rankings* and the *Times Higher Education* list also weigh international components, such as how many students and faculty are from other countries.

CONNECTING RANKINGS TO GRADUATION RATES

A college's graduation rates tend to be among the most significant categories in U.S. national rankings. However, one key point here is that these graduation rate figures are only based on the first-year students who start at the college full-time in summer or fall terms, commonly known in higher education as first-time-in-college students or first-time, full-time students. In other words, students who transfer to the college from another school or a community college are not included, nor are students who start in a spring term or who are part-time.

As you can imagine, focusing graduation rates and rankings on the subset of students who start college for the first time in the summer or fall terms can create incentives for colleges to be very deliberate about who they admit for these terms. This can, in some cases, result in not accepting students who have lower standardized test scores or a higher perceived risk of not graduating, or deferring some students to start at later terms that are not counted in the rankings.

In addition, graduation rates typically only consider students who graduated from the same college in which they originally enrolled. In other words, if a student starts at a 4-year college but then transfers to another college after their second year, they are recorded as a non-graduate from the college at which they originally started, negatively impacting the original college's graduation rates. Furthermore, in rankings systems such as *U.S. News & World Report*, a college's score for graduation rates is generally based on the percentage of students who graduate in 6 years from their first fall term of college. So if a college says they have a 70% graduation rate, that generally means that 70% of the students who are in college for the first time, and who started college in the summer or fall term, will graduate from that college in 6 years.

This also means that if you search for a college online, Google and other search engines may present federal data on 6-year graduation rates, not the 4-year graduation rates. However, many students and families see college as a 4-year experience, not a 6-year one, and they want more comprehensive data, including the average time it takes students to complete a degree at the college, for all sorts of students, not just those who start as first-year students in the summer or fall term. As a result, several states and other media organizations provide data on 4-year graduation rates, as well as rates for transfer students and those who start in the spring.

EXAMINING GRADUATION RATES AND MORE

One of the most interesting measures of a college's ability to foster student success is its ability to perform against what one might project for that college's graduation rate. A 2019 interactive project by *The New York Times* uses several variables about a college's student body to predict its graduation rates, and then assesses how far above or below the college is to the actual graduation rates (Leonhardt & Chinoy, 2019). Colleges that enroll lots of students from wealthy families and with high SAT and ACT scores tend to have high predicted graduation rates, perhaps over 80% or 90%. Colleges that enroll mostly students from underrepresented backgrounds with lower test scores tend to have lower predicted rates, perhaps closer to 40% or 50%.

In some cases, colleges graduate students at far higher rates than what the data would predict; that generally means these colleges have relatively effective ecosystems for student success. The University of La Verne in California, for example, had an expected graduation rate of 53% and an actual rate of 74%, according to *The New York Times* analysis. Other colleges have far lower graduation rates than the data would suggest, which signals they have an underdeveloped or less effective ecosystem for student success.

Looking even closer at graduation rates at colleges, there are several disparities in graduation rates that often exist at colleges between their different student populations. Students from lower-income, underrepresented backgrounds, or who are the first in their families to attend college (also known as first-generation students) often graduate at lower rates than their peers at many institutions. These disparities may be rooted in challenges from colleges and communities not designed to adequately educate and support students as they navigate financial, academic, or personal obstacles. At some colleges, particularly those without robust student engagement and community-building, out-of-state students may experience lower graduation rates as they encounter challenges in transitioning and developing a sense of belonging at the college.

However, we can see some colleges that have erased graduation rate gaps between the populations of their student body. Georgia State University in Atlanta, for instance, has been nationally recognized for its work in elevating graduation rates and erasing disparities for its large, lower-income student population (McMurtrie, 2018). Georgia State University used a comprehensive approach to rapidly mature its student success ecosystem, developing several interventions, new support and engagement programs, and financial aid programs. Colleges like Georgia State University have shown that demographics are not destiny—that it's possible for students of all backgrounds to reach graduation.

Colleges may have disparities in dimensions other than their overall graduation rate. Some colleges may trumpet their overall graduation rate, but the time it takes their students to earn their degree may vary considerably. While some students may graduate in 4 years, many others may take closer to 6 years. The average time to graduation may also vary widely among programs or majors at a college, with engineering or STEM programs often taking longer for students to complete than others.

The graduation rates and time to complete a degree for students who transfer to a bachelor's granting college from a 2-year college also vary widely. Often these are advertised as 4-year pathways: 2 years at a community college and then 2 years at a bachelor's-granting college. In practice, however, it may be 2+3 years, 2+4 years, or 2+ not graduating at all. Nationally, about 30% of students who start at a community college transfer to a 4-year college, and of those about 44% graduate in 6 years (National Student Clearinghouse Research Center, 2019a). In addition, students may spend more than 2 years at a community college before transferring to a 4-year college. Understanding how the average time to graduation varies across and within colleges can be important in evaluating institutions.

Another dimension of disparity may occur after students graduate from college. Some students thrive after graduation, while others sputter and struggle to start their career. The wide differences in what happens with students after graduation has prompted questions about what colleges should be aiming for in students' postgraduation lives. Should colleges, for instance, aim for all their students to have high salaries after graduation? State governments often reward colleges for producing graduates who are employed and earn high salaries.

If we have a student who takes a job on Wall Street with Goldman Sachs making a six-figure salary, and a student who takes a job as a teacher making under $40,000, is one student less of a success than the other? Or if we have a student who chooses to be a stay-at-home father after graduation, is that not a success? Some colleges are much better than others at ensuring students successfully enter the next phase of their lives. There isn't one right path for students to take, as success can look different for each student. Regardless of what students pursue, their life after graduation should enhance themselves and their communities. Colleges should prepare and support students toward that aim. Since this is such an important outcome of the college journey, how students fare after graduation should be considered closely.

ACCEPTANCE RATES, SELECTIVITY, AND OUTCOMES

Many students view a college's acceptance rates, or the percent of applicants the college accepts, as an informal metric to assess the popularity of the institution, their chances of getting accepted, and whether the college is prestigious enough for them. Students may assume that the fewer people accepted to the college, the better, right? However, one challenge with using acceptance or selectivity rates alone is that they can be manipulated or vary considerably by the size of the college or regional contexts or policies. A college can, for instance, drum up application numbers, offering application fee waivers and using clever marketing in order to quickly boost the number of applications it receives, or even change the size of an admitted cohort of first-year students to impact its selectivity rates. Admitting low rates of students can be a sign of prestige, but it can also deter students, perhaps first-generation ones, from applying since they may think they won't get in. As a result, rankings agencies, such as *U.S. News & World Report*, no longer consider selectivity rates in their rankings methodology. Most important, selectivity by itself doesn't predict your individual likelihood of having success at a college. In other words, a college admitting very few of its applicants does not guarantee success for the individual students who do attend.

Does the exclusivity of a college affect life after graduation for its students? A review of research on the long-term outcomes of college graduates, including from the most selective schools, has found that the selectivity of a college by itself is not a reliable predictor of student learning, job satisfaction, or well-being (Challenge Success, 2018). While highly selective schools with largely affluent and high-scoring students do have high graduation rates, there is less clarity in longer-term outcomes. For instance, this research shows that high-achieving students who ultimately decide to attend a less selective college have similar outcomes to their peers who attend a highly selective college. For example, both groups of students are equally likely to be satisfied in their job (Challenge Success, 2018).

That said, researchers do find some modest financial gains in salary for those who attend highly selective schools, with more pronounced gains for first-generation and other underrepresented students (Challenge Success, 2018). While, of course, average salaries can vary from institution to institution, these researchers found that the variation among an institution's graduates tends to be even larger. Beyond the selectivity of a college, student engagement, such as time in student organizations, in internships and major projects, studying, and more, tends to be associated with stronger long-term impacts.

As a result of these findings, some researchers conclude that the wise investment is to focus on engaging more in educationally purposeful activities while in college, and to spend less time worried about a college's selectivity. In other words, what you do in college is more important than where you go. At the same time, student engagement doesn't occur in a vacuum. What opportunities and support are available, how one spends their time and engages with the college, and even reaching graduation itself can be highly influenced by the college one attends, as this book illustrates.

CRITICISM OF RANKINGS

Due to their methodologies, *U.S. News & World Report* and other similar rankings have faced considerable criticism over the years. Opponents have argued that the rankings don't measure the quality of the entire institution or the student experience, and are biased and inaccurate. They claim, among other things, that rankings are designed to maintain the prestige of Ivy League and similar institutions with high resources.

Some of the most forceful objections have been that the existing rankings systems prize exclusivity and create incentives for colleges to deny enrollment to many students they see as "at-risk," or those who may adversely affect a college's profile: typically lower-income, first-generation, and other underrepresented students. Critics argue that since SAT and ACT scores are highly correlated to a student's family income, with students from higher incomes scoring higher on the tests, the way tests are used in admissions decisions is unfair. In this view, admissions decisions that heavily rely on standardized test scores can exacerbate social inequality.

Alternative rankings in the United States, such as the *Washington Monthly* or *Kiplinger's Best Value Colleges*, have emerged to try and address these objections, with a more explicit focus on social mobility, cost, or value. These rankings have a stronger focus on rewarding colleges for their success in enrolling and graduating students from lower-income families or for keeping costs low while still offering quality.

Beyond overall college rankings, groups such as *U.S. News & World Report* and others also rank specific academic programs at colleges, such as engineering, business, and education. The methodology varies widely in how these are calculated. For some, the rankings are based 100% on a survey of the perspectives of leaders in those fields, which privileges certain legacy programs and doesn't necessarily evaluate colleges' actual performance. For others, it is based on several input and output measures, similar to the methodology used for ranking entire colleges. Smaller and less common programs, like artistic fields in film, theater, and dance, have even less clarity on which rankings should be followed, especially since there isn't rigorous or widely accepted methodology in place.

Because so many potential students pay attention to rankings, they can create enormous pressure for colleges. This pressure can result in tension as colleges try to balance desires for high rankings, prestige, and a high-profile student body, while navigating space and budget constraints. Public colleges in particular can face tensions in crafting a student body that is seen as high achieving and is likely to graduate, while also maintaining access for a broad population.

In the end, there is no perfect ranking system; inevitably something isn't measured or can't be measured, or the weighting is inappropriate. The calculations often place outsize importance on measures like standardized test scores that are often correlated to race and socio-economic status. But that doesn't mean these rankings have no value to consumers and those seeking guidance on colleges. Consider them a possible starting point in the journey, or a perspective to consider, but to be approached with a healthy skepticism. As *U.S. News & World Report* frames it, students shouldn't choose their college solely off the rankings: "The rankings are a start, not the answer. They should be used as one tool in anyone's college search process" (Morse, 2019).

FINDING DATA IN THE COLLEGE SEARCH

At the most basic level, you should ensure the college is accredited. In the United States, accreditation from federally sanctioned organizations such as the Southern Association of Colleges and Schools and the Western Association of Schools and Colleges is foundational. Accreditation ensures that a college meets acceptable levels of quality, and it is required for the college to receive federal financial aid funds and many other forms of support. Some individual academic programs within a college may also have accreditation, through organizations like the Accreditation Board for Engineering and Technology (ABET) or the Association to Advance Collegiate Schools of Business (AACSB). While significant, accreditation does not automatically mean high quality, and this book looks deeper at the colleges to help evaluate beyond accreditation.

Getting good, unbiased data to compare institutions across the many dimensions of student success is challenging. After all, some elements of the college experience are subjective or difficult to standardize. How would one accurately assess students' intellectual development, for instance, across the many different courses and colleges?

Some have argued that results from national student surveys, such as the National Survey of Student Engagement and the College Senior Survey, would be better ways to compare the learning at various colleges. These surveys assess student activities at colleges, such as engagement with their professors and peers and perceptions of learning and growth. While the data from these surveys are not publicly available, colleges may be willing to share their data if asked. Some even promote their results in their recruitment materials. In addition, colleges may have their own surveys they administer to students or alumni to assess longer-term impacts of their college experiences. The results of these surveys are often publicized by the college.

The federal government tracks graduation rates and a host of other student success data for the public. The National Center for Education Statistics' College Navigator website (nces.ed.gov/collegenavigator/)

provides a quick way to review the data for virtually any college. There you can access information about a college, including its academic offerings, enrollment, costs, financial aid, and the graduation rate performance for a range of students, including by gender, race and ethnicity, and income. You can also view the federal government's College Scorecard (collegescorecard.ed.gov), which aggregates much of this information, and includes other dimensions including salaries of graduates. College Scorecard and other federal websites have been criticized for prioritizing salary data of graduates and not including other data about life after graduation that citizens may want to know. However, these websites can be helpful resources in gathering data that would otherwise be hard to find and aggregate.

The Student Achievement Measure (SAM, www.studentachievementmeasure.org) is another resource that has graduation rate data for many colleges managed by the Association of Public and Land-grant Universities. SAM was created, in part, to respond to limitations in the U.S. government and other national reporting on graduation rates. Specifically, the SAM captures both students who graduated from a college and those who transferred to other colleges and graduated from them. Because the SAM data are more inclusive, the graduation rates for each college in the SAM are higher than in the government and rankings data.

The SAM data are accessible to the public, and include how many students transferred out from each college. However, the SAM does not reveal why students left a college to transfer to another college; it may be that students were unhappy at the college because of poor instruction and that potential students should be cautious about attending it. For these reasons, some observers discount the SAM, but it can be another helpful tool for getting a full picture of a college.

Outside of national data sources, certain state systems of public higher education may be important sources of data and information. These systems may display data of interest on their websites. For instance, the University of California System (www.universityof-california.edu/infocenter) and the State University System of Florida (www.flbog.edu/resources/data-analytics/dashboards) both surface important data about institutional performance, student success, and different activities for their colleges. Along with robust data about individual public colleges, such portals also provide important general information or trend data about higher education in the state. For example, the University of California system displays data about alumni of the system, such as what kind of jobs they get, the social mobility enabled by the college, and more.

You can also get data from individual colleges, either through direct inquiry or by finding it on their websites. Most colleges have a central institutional research office which will display data about the college with lots of details. Many colleges also display their submission to something called the Common Data Set (www.commondataset.org), which can be found by searching a college's name and "Common Data Set." The Common Data Set initiative uses a standardized form that compiles much of the information about a college that is then used by ranking groups and media organizations to produce their publications. By reviewing the CDS for a college yourself, you can see data without the filter or spin of different media organizations. If so inclined, you can pay *U.S. News & World Report* and other organizations for access to more data about the colleges they rank.

The important thing is to look deeply at each institution. Examine the graduation rates, both between colleges and within colleges. Understand what disparities might exist among the different student populations of a college: Do students from lower incomes graduate at the same high rates as those who have more money? If you are planning on going to a 2-year college and then transferring for a bachelor's degree, understand the success rates at both colleges and how long students generally take to graduate from each institution.

Even with all this, there will still be more data that you will want about colleges and more questions you'll want answered. As we go through the book and examine different dimensions of higher education, we'll learn more about what colleges do and how to ask for and assess information directly.

THREE GUIDING QUESTIONS TO ASK ABOUT A COLLEGE'S DATA

1. To what extent does the college graduate its students in a timely way?
2. To what extent, if at all, are there disparities in graduation rates across its student populations or majors?
3. To what extent do students at the college have strong postgraduation outcomes?

Table 2.1. A Rubric for Evaluating a College's Performance Data

Level	Indicators
Excellent	College has exceptionally high 4- and 6-year graduation rates with virtually no disparities in rates among the student population, exceeding predicted graduation rates; college has strong postgraduation outcomes with students securing appropriate further education or employment; students report strong, positive learning and development from their college experience.
Good	College has 4- and 6-year graduation rates that exceed national averages and predicted rates for the college; small disparities exist between student populations; college has relatively strong postgraduation outcomes with students securing appropriate further education or employment, though gaps are present among the graduates.
Average	College has graduation rates that are about the national average and on par with predicted rates, though some disparities remain among student populations and between majors, as well as among students' postgraduation outcomes; students report mixed levels of learning and development from their college experience.
Fair	College outcomes are below the national average and a college's predicted graduation rate, with large disparities present between student groups and different majors, as well as among students' postgraduation outcomes.
Poor	College has low 4- and 6-year graduation rates, with wide disparities among the student body, particularly among underserved student populations, as well as among students' postgraduation outcomes; significant percentages of students report limited learning and growth from their college experience.

Part II

EXCELLING ACADEMICALLY

CHAPTER 3

The Curriculum

What Happens in the Classroom Matters

Imagine you're deciding your major and registering for courses. Your college, like many others, does this process online; you log on to your college's website and make your selection from a series of lists. First, you pick your major. You face a sea of options, with increasingly specific subfields. There's engineering, which is broken down into industrial engineering, mechanical engineering, biomedical engineering, and so on. Or there's English, with majors in literature, editing, and creative writing. When you go to sign up for classes, the sheer number of offerings within each field is dizzying. Some of these courses are only offered online or once a year. Other courses take the form of large lectures or are taught through small discussion groups.

Given how many choices there are, how can you decide? How can you make sense of the curriculum?

Teaching can be one of the most powerful, transformative things colleges do. It has enormous potential; when you are learning you are changing your mind, your brain, and the decisions you make. Learning allows us to develop new skills and perspectives and to approach problems differently. When we learn, our assumptions about ourselves and the world are examined and re-evaluated. But colleges must work to realize their students' potential, to design themselves and their learning environments, particularly in the classroom, for this kind of impact.

The curriculum is the set of academic courses students take. Curriculums vary based on the requirements of a student's major or degree, as we will explore later in this chapter. Moreover, curriculums are the core of the college experience and present unique opportunities for growth. They reflect key learning outcomes of an institution: What does a college want their students to know and be able to do once they leave the college? Taking and completing a set of courses is what earns students a degree. Without completing a curriculum, students would not graduate. On the surface, this all seems straightforward. Students look at the set of courses for a degree, say for a biology major, take them in somewhat specific order, then graduate, right?

Unfortunately, the majors and courses, and the ways in which students make decisions, progress, and learn through curriculums are often much more complicated. Not all courses and curriculums are the same, and there is enormous variation in the quality of the design, delivery, and teaching of courses. Too often courses are managed poorly and taught in ways that fail to fully harness learning opportunities, hindering students' development and progress to graduation and beyond.

In this chapter we will explore some guiding principles to help you assess a college's course offerings and their implications for student success.

DEVELOPING A LEARNING PERSPECTIVE

Learning is more than rote memorization; learning is making and re-making the meaning of the world. It includes developing our ability to think critically, the capacity to understand the world from the perspectives of others, and the notion that one can and should grow. Accordingly, learning should be thought of as an active process that goes beyond just the years a student spends in college. As students encounter changing circumstances, develop interests and relationships, and embark on initiatives, they should continue to learn.

This kind of expansive perspective on learning is important for student development in college. If students start college with this viewpoint, they can better take ownership of their learning, and make connections between their different courses and out-of-class experiences. Key to this perspective is having specific learning mindsets around growth.

Someone with a *growth mindset* understands that intelligence is not fixed; it's not that some people are inherently "bad" at math, for instance. People have the capacity to learn and grow. In this light, the effort of trying to solve math problems makes any student better, regardless of whether they solved the problem correctly the first time. A growth mindset is critical for students to step outside their comfort zones, set high expectations for themselves, and truly realize their potential. A student with this mindset can thus see college as a chance to experiment, take intellectual risks, learn from errors, and grow from testing their limits.

Developing a growth mindset magnifies student learning and performance and helps to close gaps in student success (Stephens et al., 2014). Many colleges recognize the role they can play in helping students develop this kind of learning perspective. The University of Texas at Austin, for example, seeks to cultivate a growth mindset right away with its students, having incoming students read and engage with stories from former students, who offer advice for overcoming the challenges that they faced during their time in college, resulting in positive academic impacts on the students in their first year of college (EAB, 2019). For some students, a bad grade or big fight with a friend can completely derail their academic careers and sense of belonging at a college. But students with growth mindsets are able to dust themselves off, recognizing that a bad event or grade doesn't define them.

While it is incumbent on students to develop a growth mindset and learning perspective, colleges geared toward student success will also take steps to cultivate these attitudes. As we'll discuss in the next section, excellent courses foster these mindsets and perspectives in order to create the conditions for student learning and success.

WHAT IS A GOOD COURSE?

In the movies, a college course is often portrayed as a large classroom with a professor standing in front of the room, lecturing, and the students busily taking down notes so that they may memorize the material for some future exam or test. Unfortunately, this was, and still is, the reality for too many courses.

In the last few decades, experts have learned much about how students develop and learn, and what teaching approaches can help students thrive, regardless of racial, class, and ethnic backgrounds. They found that the stereotypical model where students just passively listen to a professor lecturing, also known as the instructor-centered approach, is rarely optimal for student learning. As Chickering and Gamson (1987) write, "Learning is not a spectator sport . . . [Students] must talk about what they are learning, write about it, relate it to past experiences, apply it to their daily lives. They must make what they learn part of themselves" (p. 4).

Frequently, professors continue an instructor-centered model because it's what they know—they were taught that way and often don't have training or experiences in other approaches. Teaching from this model, however, can easily result in poor outcomes for the student.

While not necessarily the case, these instructor-centered approaches are often less likely to produce optimal outcomes for students compared to *learner-centered teaching approaches*, which we will discuss more below.

Failing many students is seen by some professors as a way to preserve rigor in a course, or to "weed out" weak students who they think shouldn't be in the college or shouldn't be studying in a particular major. In fact, at many colleges with instructor-centered models of teaching, it is not unusual to see a third or even more of the students in a course not pass, particularly in first-year math or science courses, with significant disparities by race, gender, or income of students. When so many of the students regularly fail a course, there is a problem with the design of the course itself.

Take for example Emma, a current junior, who entered her college as an Engineering major. Students considered the program especially difficult because of weed-out courses. During her sophomore year, Emma began taking classes within the department. "I felt set up to fail," Emma said. She described a class that she felt was intentionally designed to be exceedingly difficult. The teaching style was exclusively based around jargon-heavy lectures, and the professor rarely paused for student questions. When the professor quizzed the students, the questions he asked did not correlate to the readings or lectures, giving them little opportunity to demonstrate their knowledge.

The professor seemed to assume that Emma and her peers already had a high-level knowledge of engineering, when the course was supposed to be introductory. Emma, along with many other students, didn't pass the course. She viewed her final low grade in the class as a reflection of a lack of intellect, revealing that she was not smart enough to succeed in the program and not meant to be an engineer at all. This experience profoundly impacted how she viewed herself and how she interacted with her college. Emma dropped out of the Engineering program and was so demoralized that she struggled to decide on a new area of study.

As Emma's story shows, when professors are not learner-centered, they often don't maximize learning and can even exacerbate inequality. Teaching that isn't learner-centered tends to favor the students who enter college with backgrounds and resources that prime them for success. Understanding that students can grow is particularly important when you have students in a course who have various levels of preparation prior to taking it. After all, not all students arrive at college with the same understanding, skill sets, and existing knowledge.

Some students, for instance, may have come from a lower-income rural community that didn't offer much beyond basic-level math in high school. As Supiano (2018) writes:

> College students aren't blank slates. They have spent years acquiring an excellent education, or a crummy one. They have been encouraged by the adults in their lives, or they have been undermined. Long before they arrive on campus, they have the assurance that the world is theirs for the taking, or the knowledge that their intelligence and worth will be questioned at every turn because of where they come from or what their parents do or the color of their skin.

Professors and colleges have a responsibility to try and create the optimal conditions for student learning to occur. As experts in their various academic fields, professors should see themselves as engineers of student learning; they are the ones who create the conditions for all students to learn and grow.

In the last decades, research has suggested, and some colleges have begun to put into practice, different approaches that produce better outcomes for students. While we can't examine all the nuances of teaching and the associated research here, there are a few evidence-based guiding principles to look for in college courses and teaching.

First, the college should use *learner-centered teaching approaches* to help students achieve learning goals, rather than simply instructor-centered ones. Generally, this means that the instructor shifts the focus of a course's activity away from the instructor and toward the student. Learner-centered instruction in colleges takes many forms and often uses active rather than passive learning strategies. Instead of passively sitting listening to content being delivered in a lecture, with little to no interaction, students actively engage with each other and the instructor. Small groups and projects empower conversation and perspective-sharing among the students, giving them ownership of the learning process. In many large courses, you see graduate students or trained undergraduates, also known as "teaching assistants" or "learning assistants," facilitating these discussions or efforts. In courses with active learning, students often learn more and feel more connected (Nilson, 2016).

Interestingly, research has found that students often think they learn more when the course is taught by traditional lecture-based approaches rather than in active learning courses. It may feel more comfortable for a student to sit in a passive lecture, listen to the instructor for the class session, and call that learning. But an active-learning model, which forces the student to engage with gaps in their knowledge during class, may make the student feel like they aren't learning as much (Deslauriers et al., 2019). But this same research finds that students' performance and actual learning is significantly higher in active learning courses, and that more students in a course have higher levels of achievement. Active learning approaches call on students to be more engaged and present during class, which means students are doing the work of learning, even if it pushes them out of their comfort zones (Freeman et al., 2014).

Learner-centered teaching is especially important in gateway courses, which are generally taught during the first or second year of college. These gateway courses are the students' first introduction to a discipline, and they are typically the required courses to move forward toward a major (also known in college as prerequisite courses). Biology 101, for example, is a "gateway" into the broader biology field.

Learner-centered teaching, particularly active learning strategies, is especially impactful in science, technology, engineering, and math (STEM) courses in the first and second years of college, where it is common that professors use instructor-centered models with little active student engagement. To put it plainly, students, especially those from underrepresented populations, do not do as well in these instructor-centered courses (Theobald et al., 2020). Students learn less, and they may even leave a major because they think they are not good at math or science or whatever subject. In fact, students in STEM courses are *1.5 times more likely* to fail a course if it uses traditional lecturing compared to one that uses active-learning approaches (Freeman et al., 2014).

Regardless of their students' disciplines, the college should understand how critical it is for students to succeed in early gateway courses: not only to gain confidence in their abilities, and to continue to subsequent courses, but to strengthen their foundational skills so that they perform well in later courses and in their careers.

A second principle of a good course is having a *syllabus* that clearly articulates how students will be changed by the conclusion: What will students be able to do at the end that they couldn't do at the beginning, and what will they have learned? How will that be measured? How will students demonstrate their learning? Professors should then design the course to achieve the goals and outcomes outlined in the syllabus. The learning outcomes of the course should be connected to and build upon the other courses in an academic program, preparing students to do well as they progress in college.

Third, professors should give special attention to curating an *inclusive learning climate*. Such an environment fosters participation, intellectual growth, broadening of perspectives, and success of all students. As the Center for the Advancement of Teaching (CAT, 2019b) at Florida State University reminds professors:

> Humans are social mammals, so our learning is profoundly influenced by our social and emotional context. When we feel welcomed and respected, we can be open to new experiences. We feel safe to engage, and we can exert our higher-order cognitive powers, so we can stretch intellectually. If we feel threatened, or alienated, or anxious, on the other hand, our cognitive abilities are curtailed, and we're far less likely to be curious or reflective. (n.p.)

Classroom climates that are stressful or unwelcoming (also known in higher education as "chilly classroom climates") can negatively impact student learning, especially for students who are underrepresented in academic environments, like women in many STEM courses or students who are minorities at colleges that primarily enroll students who are White (Pascarella et al., 1997; Schulze & Tomal, 2006).

Thus, if you are visiting college classes as a potential student, you will want to consider the teaching style and climate of the classes. You'll want to look for signals that the professor truly sees and cares about their students. Practices such as "immediacy" help students feel close and connected with the instructor and peers. Immediacy can be seen through how the professor interacts with the students, such as by making friendly eye contact or calling on students by name. A professor who practices immediacy may also move around the classroom, arrive early to talk with students, and stay after for additional questions (CAT, 2019b).

You may also sense a professor's enthusiasm for the topic and for teaching; researchers have found that an instructor's enthusiasm can be contagious, helping provide intrinsic and positive motivation for students to engage with the course (Patrick et al., 2000). You may see how comfortable and valued the students seem in the class, and that there is a welcoming environment for them to ask questions and explore ideas. Courses should be taught with equity and cultural diversity in mind, so look for whether the instructor uses inclusive language, course materials, and practices when engaging and learning with students. By doing so, these courses seek "to equalize opportunity for students for all backgrounds to participate and succeed in class" (Supiano, 2018).

Fourth, you should examine what *expectations* instructors have for their students. Effective instruction sets high expectations for students, championing a growth mindset. Researchers have found that when professors believe in growth mindsets—that students can improve academically—students in their courses tend to do better and be more motivated, with fewer disparities between demographic groups (Canning et al., 2019). These expectations can be communicated in a variety of ways, such as an instructor's verbal and nonverbal cues. A patient tone, encouraging facial expression, or choice of words can bolster students' confidence and engagement, while clearly communicating expectations (CAT, 2019b). High expectations can also be communicated by statements that suggest a student is capable of high achievement. Conversely, if a professor uses rhetoric that only serves to set low expectations for the course, one can be skeptical of the course truly centering student success.

Charlie was taking a course on the ethics of biochemistry, which was outside of his comfort zone. As a chemistry major, he normally took courses with labs and practical application of theories, but he wanted to try taking something that would challenge him. One of the major assignments for the class was an analytical essay, which asked the students to research how morality in biochemistry had evolved over the previous decades. Charlie was used to writing lab reports, not longer papers, and was feeling anxious about tackling the assignment. About 2 weeks before the paper was due, the professor started class by discussing the assignment. She pulled up the assignment description from the syllabus and spent a few minutes going through its components. She then addressed the class, telling them that she had complete confidence in their ability to complete the assignment, and she was impressed by their quality of work so far. Charlie, listening, felt reassured that this assignment was within his capabilities. When he finally started writing his essay, he kept going back to the expectations his professor had laid out, and he used that to give him confidence and motivation.

Fifth, effective instruction also provides frequent and formative *feedback* to students and asks them to regularly reflect on their learning. In *How Learning Works* Susan Ambrose and colleagues explain that learning results from "goal-directed practice coupled with targeted feedback" (Ambrose et al., 2010, p. 125). Effective feedback "(a) communicates to students where they are relative to the stated goals and what they need to do to improve and (b) provides this information to students when they can make the most use of it" (CAT, 2019a). Too often, however, feedback in courses comes too late in the process for students to learn from it. In order to foster a culture of growth, an instructor might consult with students individually to give detailed feedback on essays, rather than just assigning grades. Additionally, the professor may spend class time going over commonly missed exam questions to fill in gaps in their learning.

There is evidence that having instructors who are diverse and look like the students they are teaching can advance student success for the entire student body, enriching teaching and learning in a number of ways (Hagedorn et al., 2007; Marx & Goff, 2005). Having professors who come from diverse backgrounds, and who serve as mentors for students, can also help students feel less like imposters in college and more that they belong at the institution (Hurtado, 2001). Thus, evaluating the diversity of the professors of a college can be a significant dimension when evaluating a college, not just for students of color but for all students who will benefit from the diversity of perspectives.

Every instructor has the capacity to be effective, as long as they deploy evidence-based teaching practices. Professors (and the college as a whole) should see themselves as partners with the students in their success. In short, if the course is designed well, with the right support and engagement, students can succeed at higher rates, and learn much more, particularly students underrepresented in higher education.

COMPONENTS OF A COURSE:
TESTS, GROUP PROJECTS, AND MORE

Now that we have a broad understanding of what makes a good course, let's think about the role of a few common, specific components of a course.

First, we'll look at tests and assessments. Whatever their teaching approach, professors still need to assess student learning. In addition to traditional exams, instructors might assign projects, papers, group assignments, and presentations. Regardless of the shape assessment takes, it must be well-designed so that students can demonstrate their learning and mastery of course material. Some colleges have an over-reliance on high-stakes testing, in which a single test accounts for a large percentage of a student's grade. This can amplify student anxiety, gives students fewer opportunities to get feedback on their progress, and limits opportunities for demonstration of learning. On the other hand, frequent, low-stakes assessments, such as weekly quizzes or reflection assignments, allow for regular check-ups on understanding and the opportunity to receive feedback. Low-stakes assessments also encourage students to review class material continuously, rather than waiting until the final exam. Because these smaller assignments do not count for a significant part of a course grade, students have room to make mistakes without feeling high amounts of pressure. Failing one small assignment won't derail a student's grade and demotivate them from the learning process.

Communication is a fundamental skill. Courses should provide opportunities for students to write intensively, present their work, and receive sufficient feedback on their writing. Writing-intensive college courses have been found to be a high-impact practice; that is, they significantly contribute to students' learning, development, and academic performance (Kuh, 2008). However, many college courses can only offer limited writing assignments because of the high cost in time and attention for instructors to give feedback and grade significant writing assignments. Colleges that focus on student success, and that have a conception of success that includes the full development of students, will require students to take at least some courses with significant writing components. Prospective students should seek out colleges that provide these growth opportunities for students.

Collaborative assignments and cooperative projects can be particularly impactful in student development with a host of positive outcomes that promote student learning and success. As outlined by Kuh (2008), collaborative assignments and projects combine two key goals: "Learning to work and solve problems in the company of others, and sharpening one's own understanding by listening seriously to the insights of others, especially those with different backgrounds and life experiences" (p. 9). Companies around the world use teams to accomplish tasks, so cultivating skills to work well in groups will be valued by employers (Bughin et al., 2018). Group projects can also help build students' social networks, which can have a positive impact on mental health, as we will explore later in the book.

Given all these considerations, what does an excellently designed course actually look like? One example comes from Worcester Polytechnic Institute's Great Problems Seminar (www.wpi.edu/academics/undergraduate/great-problems-seminar). The course asks first-year students to work collaboratively together on project-based learning on real-world challenges that are of great importance, like food sustainability and complex issues involved in how we feed a growing world population. While these projects may seem intimidating, the instructors set high expectations for students and empower them to work creatively on these large issues. Students engage in research and inquiry, working throughout the course individually and in teams answering questions and proposing ideas, culminating in student presentations at the end of the course. The course combines classroom learning with practical application, such that students see the value in what they do. The Seminar strongly cultivates a sense of purpose in its students; according to one survey, alumni of the program report that the course contributed to a high sense of confidence about their capacity to effect positive change in the world (Dedman, 2019).

HOW MANY CLASSES SHOULD YOU TAKE?

For many years in higher education, colleges recommended that students take a light course load when they first start college to give them time to adjust. Typically, this meant starting college with a schedule of 12 credit hours per semester, instead of 15 or more. In a two-semester system, which separates the academic year into fall and spring semesters, 12 credit hours would mean taking four classes each semester. (While some colleges use quarters or blocks, the two-semester system is the norm.) The U.S. Department of Education sets a 12-credit-hour minimum to be considered a full-time student for financial aid purposes, which helped establish this course load as a common starting place. But what does the data say is the best courseload for student performance?

Instead of taking a lighter, 12-credit-hour courseload, the research has generally found that full-time students should take 15 or more credit hours per semester, and start doing so from their first semester in college (Venit, 2017). Students who take 15 or more hours per semester are more likely to stay in college and have higher grades than their peers who take fewer credits. Research has found this across a variety of backgrounds; students benefited from taking 15 credits regardless of income levels or their achievement in high school. The research also finds that students who start college with a higher courseload continue to take a similar number of classes each subsequent semester. Conversely, students who begin by taking a lower number of credit hours tend to keep taking that same amount. In other words, if a student takes only 12 credit hours their first semester, it's unlikely they'll take 15 in the future. They are more likely to extend their time in college to complete degree requirements, if they graduate at all (Venit, 2017).

Why does taking more classes generally produce better academic results? First, it keeps students busy and engaged in productive, educational spaces, helping give structure and formation to students' days without leaving too much discretionary time. As students move from relatively structured environments of high school to less structured environments of college, being busy with courses can help provide the daily regularity and structure that helps students thrive. Second, students generally need to take 15 credit hours per semester to graduate within 4 years. The standard total credit hours for a U.S. bachelor's degree is 120 credit hours, which equals 15 credit hours across eight semesters, unless the students take summer courses every year or arrive at college with lots of accelerated credit. If a student takes only 12 credit hours each fall and spring for all 4 years, they're taking 96 credit hours total—falling far short of the needed 120. The longer students stay in college, the higher the costs and the increased possibility that life circumstances will change in ways that can derail students (Vandal, 2019).

At some colleges, there are informational and advising campaigns to encourage students to register for 15 credit hours per term, such as the University of Hawaii's 15 to Finish campaign, while other colleges simply advocate for students to take 30 credit hours per academic year to ensure timely graduation. Many colleges also have tuition pricing models that encourage students to take more credit hours, such as a flat-rate tuition, which allow students to take more than 12 credit hours without incurring additional costs. Some colleges provide additional funding for students that take 15 hours, such as California's Community Colleges' Student Success Completion Grant. Other scholarship programs, such as the New Mexico Legislative Lottery Scholarship, require students to take 15 credit hours per semester.

Of course, there should be upper limits to the number of credit hours a student can take within a semester, and many colleges do (or should have) limits on the maximum number of credit hours a student can take in a semester. If a student wants to take more than 18 credit hours or six classes, they often need explicit permission from the college to do so. An overzealous and confident student may be tempted to register for six courses in their first term in college, including some advanced courses designed for seniors, only to be overwhelmed by the amount of work required, with negative academic consequences.

Advising at the college, discussed in more detail in Chapter 4, should help students build optimal course schedules that include appropriate level and number of courses. A student may have personal or academic circumstances that make taking a full course load of 15 credit hours difficult or even impossible. A skilled advisor can help students navigate these challenges.

ARE THERE ENOUGH COURSES?

Unfortunately, it's common for colleges to fail to offer enough courses or large enough courses for their students. This typically occurs because a college doesn't have enough resources, doesn't align their resources well with student needs, or doesn't plan student enrollments accurately. Students often struggle when they encounter this, causing undue stress or even delaying when some complete their degree.

Let's consider Amy, a Literature major, who was required to take a senior seminar course in her last semester in college. She was in the first group of students able to sign up for classes, starting at 8:00 A.M. By 8:02, the senior seminar was already full. The problem was not that Amy slept in too late, or didn't plan ahead, but that the college did not offer enough spots in the class for the students who needed it to graduate. Amy remembers desperately posting to different online forums, begging other students to let her take their spot in the class. She went so far as to offer money, but no one responded to her postings or messages. She went to her college advisor, but they told her it would be impossible to offer another section of the course, given their limited professors and resources. With no way of taking the senior seminar, Amy was forced to extend her time at college and take the course in the next semester.

As Amy's story demonstrates, students often can't get the courses they need, in the term they need them, to make progress toward a 4-year degree. In addition to a lack of spots (also referred to as seats), another problem may be that courses are offered at conflicting times. Students may struggle if two required classes are offered at the same time on Tuesday mornings. Courses may also not be reflective of students' diverse needs. If a college enrolls many working adults, but offers classes only during business hours, students may be forced to compromise between their job and their education.

Moreover, some courses may be offered only once per year, which can result in students struggling to enroll. If a student enrolled in such a course doesn't pass, or has to withdraw from the semester because of illness, the consequences are severe. Instead of simply retaking the course the following semester, they have to wait an entire year, possibly delaying timely graduation. Imagine getting to your very last semester, not being able to take a required course, and having to stay in college for another year, as Amy was forced to do! Sometimes professors dictate when they want to teach, rather than considering when students need the courses. In colleges with this instructor-centered outlook, the majority of classes might be offered in the same time slots that are preferable only to professors. These factors, among others, inhibit students from building a productive class schedule to make progress toward a degree.

It is important to look through colleges' course offerings to be sure they offer key courses often enough, distributed over the day and week, and with sufficient seats for students. In other words, look for a college that has a more student-centered approach to scheduling and offering courses. Asking students at the campus if they can get the courses they need, when they need them, can give you important insights. Likewise, asking a college department, such as engineering, directly about course availability can be a good approach—and it will let the college know that people, particularly prospective students and their families, are paying close attention to this issue.

IS CLASS SIZE IMPORTANT?

The number of students in a course can vary widely. Some classes have fewer than 10 students, while others may have hundreds of students. There are many reasons for this variation. At many institutions, having professors teach small classes is expensive, and it certainly costs more than having professors teach large classes with lots of students. It's especially common for introductory courses to be larger, and for class size to shrink as students proceed in their major and find specializations. National rankings encourage colleges to consider class size. *U.S. News & World Report*, for example, values class size highly, giving colleges who have more small classes more points in their rankings. They define small as under 50 students and give the most weight to courses with fewer than 20 students. Colleges with smaller courses think it matters too, frequently touting their course sizes and student-to-faculty ratios to prospective students.

There is not especially robust research on the impact of class size on student learning and well-being. Researchers do see improvements in student course completion rates in smaller class sizes, though it's unclear what exactly is the magic number (Benton & Pallett, 2013). Smaller classes can make it easier for a professor to use learner-centered and active learning strategies, and for students to feel account-able to being present and engaged in the course. It's easier for students to feel anonymous in a larger class, and to suppose that the professor doesn't care if the students engage. Some students may not bother to even show up to class, assuming that their attendance doesn't matter. Moreover, if a large lecture hall has chairs that are bolted down, it's harder to get into groups and work together on a project during class to facilitate active learning. It's also more difficult to grade more complex and perhaps more meaningful assignments in large classes without con-siderable teaching support. Without good measures to monitor student progress in large courses, students may slip through the cracks and go unnoticed, even if they need support. In smaller courses it may be easi-er to build community among fellow students and to let them feel con-nected to and mentored by the instructor, elevating students' sense of belonging and well-being. Smaller classes may also help students more easily develop relationships with their instructors, and therefore allow students to ask for quality letters of recommendation.

While some large courses are not optimal for student success, as outlined above, this is not to say that large classes are inherently bad. As you assess a college's curriculum, you should look for approaches that address some of the concerns associated with large class sizes. One example is an early alert or progress report program that triggers red flags if there is a worry about a student's performance or a sudden lack of attendance. These programs allow professors to share midterm performance with key college resources or support programs if the student consents, or to conduct a welfare check on the student.

Redesigning courses, even large courses, to make them more active learning–based has been shown to drastically improve attendance and the completion rates of courses (Nilson, 2016). These approaches can also make a large course feel smaller, with more intimate groups of students working together. One effective approach, popular in physics and other STEM courses, is the SCALE-UP model, in which students sit in chairs in small circles around round tables and work together on problems during class (Nilson, 2016). Other institutional models include the learning-assistant model, a learner-centered approach in which trained students in college are paid to help their peers in courses engage in active learning during class and to offer support to them be-yond the class time (Sellami et al., 2017).

As you consider various colleges, you can ask them directly for class size information. The data is also collected and partially displayed in *U.S. News & World Report* rankings, or you can get the data yourself from an internet search of a college's Common Data Set, which is often publicly shared by colleges and collects much of the information that rankings and media organizations use to assess colleges. (See Chapter 2 for more information.)

Class size may not be the only indicator of how much interaction a student can expect with professors and peers, however. A college's student-to-faculty ratio may be another proxy for what level of engagement a student may have with professors. Colleges often promote having a low student-to-faculty ratio, featuring it prominently on their advertisements. However, these ratios can be misleading. A ratio of 15 students to one professor at a college may seem intimate, but how exactly those professors are deployed on campus can vary widely. Some professors may spend much or most of their time on research or only teach graduate courses, which means they generally won't be teaching undergraduates. The overall ratio also may not reflect the distribution across campus in different departments. One department may have a student-to-faculty ratio that allows for small classes and lots of student–professor interaction, while another department may be over capacity and have very few professors per student leading to little student–professor contact and mentorship.

So look at the collegewide student-to-faculty ratio, take it with a grain of salt, and then dig deeper: Ask questions about the ratio in a particular department of interest, talk with professors, and then talk with students about their experiences.

GUIDED PATHWAYS: STRUCTURE AND GUIDANCE MATTERS

In high school, students have a relatively limited set of courses to choose from, but in college there can be hundreds or even thousands of courses and different programs. All of these options are part of the diverse and exploratory nature of higher education. While they allow for tremendous choice and exposure to various disciplines, the immense offerings can also have a negative impact on students. As Venit and Bevevino (2020) articulate:

> Unfettered choice creates unhelpful complexity and introduces risk for students who are just starting their college careers and not yet confident in navigating their new environments. Without proper guidance,

students can become discouraged by a lack of direction, fall victim to choice paralysis, and choose to leave school instead of persisting. Others make costly course-planning mistakes that extend graduation timelines and hinder completion. (p. 16)

To help students make productive academic choices and counter the anxiety of unfettered choice, some colleges provide *guided pathways* for their students. A guided pathway is an articulated semester-by-semester set of required courses in the curriculum that a student should sequentially move through within their major in order to graduate. It may also be referred to as an academic map or major map. These help colleges monitor student academic progress and ensure that students are on track as they progress. Often these maps lay out specific courses a student should take within a semester, or milestones they should meet.

While not all colleges have guided pathways, they are a helpful way of understanding what the college expects of its students. For the colleges that use guided pathways, their requirements and the sequencing of courses should be available for you to see. You can ask a college's department to review their guided pathways with you. Key questions include: What and how many courses are required? In what order? Does the pathway include milestones or timelines for completing various requirements? What happens if a student misses a milestone, or gets off track?

People have argued that colleges should not develop such guided pathways (Bailey, Jaggars, & Jenkins, 2015). They argue that college is a time for maximum exploration, so structure that interferes with that ought to be avoided. But as we saw in the quote from Venit and Bevenino above, too many academic options and choices can yield worse results—students, particularly underserved students, can easily get lost in the labyrinth of higher education. Guided pathways can significantly boost student success. It is a disservice to students to not offer the guidance they need to make timely progress toward a major and to provide them indications if they are not likely to be successful in a pathway. These maps constructively narrow choice; they do not eliminate it. Guided pathways still offer the exploration and freedom for students to choose among many courses and elective options. They are just providing direction to help students get to degree completion in a timely manner.

GENERAL EDUCATION COURSES

In many places, the first 2 years of college courses are largely composed of what is known as general education. General education refers to the broad set of courses the college (or the state government in some public colleges) consider to be foundational to college education and to prepare students for life. General education programs often include courses that have a focus on history, diversity, writing, math, sciences, and more. Lynn Pasquerella, president of the Association of American Colleges and Universities (AAC&U), articulates that the value of this kind of broad education is that it

> teaches them to write and speak and think with precision, coherence, and clarity; to anticipate and respond to objections, propose arguments; and to be able to engage in a moral imagination—imagining what it's like to be in the shoes of another, different from one's self. (Young, 2019)

General education gives students the wider training and skill development that promotes career readiness and full civic and intellectual engagement. A college should state the learning outcomes for students and certain competencies that should be developed from their general education requirements, and these should be measured to see if students are meeting them.

As part of the college's general education, a college may offer or require a first-year seminar course for students—typically a smaller course in which first-year students explore an issue in depth with a professor. These courses have been identified as a high-impact practice in higher education, resulting in significant learning and elevating academic performance and graduation rates (Kuh, 2008). Finding colleges with these kinds of intensive learning experiences within the general education curriculum can be an important dimension in empowering student success.

CAPSTONE COURSES AND SENIOR PROJECTS

Students are often required to take capstone courses or senior seminars in their last year of study. These courses are intended to give students an opportunity to use their accumulated knowledge from their collegiate career. These classes integrate a student's prior learning and typically ask them to produce a project or performance of some kind.

Usually, capstone or seminar courses have smaller class sizes. Many are designed to model graduate-level courses in structure and rigor. Like their first-year seminar counterparts, capstone courses and senior projects are also a high-impact practice, lifting student performance (Kuh, 2008).

The shape of these seminars may look different across different majors and disciplines. At the University of Cincinnati, for instance, students majoring in Biology can choose to pursue a research, lecture, field trip, or assistantship option for their senior seminar (University of Cincinnati, n.d.). By the end of their senior year, they will have produced a high-level paper and corresponding presentation based on their research or field work or have designed and presented laboratory lessons to their class. Humanities students studying Romance languages and literature, for instance, will participate in a capstone forum in which they present their work. This may take the form of a research essay, but it could also be an original literary work or a translation of a text.

Regardless of discipline, senior seminar courses and projects have both educational and professional benefits. Students are given the space to complete a substantive project, empowering them to develop their own ideas and have high levels of control over their learning. The final product, whether it is a research paper, a portfolio, a performance, or something else, is also useful in demonstrating students' skills and knowledge as they apply for graduate school, employment, or other postgraduation opportunities.

WHAT ABOUT ONLINE COURSES?

Online courses are common across higher education. In fact, in 2016, about one out of every three students in higher education learned online (NCES, 2017a). In Spring 2020, college campuses were closed in reaction to the COVID–19 pandemic and in-person courses rapidly moved online. In the 2020–21 academic year, continued adjustments forced by the pandemic necessitated greater use of online learning. Many online courses are taught in what is known as asynchronous models, in which every student works through the course on their own time. These models accommodate the variety of students' schedules because students do not all have to gather or participate together at the same time or place. Another approach to online courses is synchronous learning, in which video conference technology or other means are used so that students engage with each other at the same time. There are also hybrid or blended approaches, which combine online learning with in-person engagement. Students may work in online modules some days of the week, and in physical classrooms others, or may supplement the online course with extended in-person meetings throughout the term. Online courses, regardless of model, typically require high levels of self-discipline and strong time management skills, which students are developing throughout their time in college. Because many first-year students haven't had much practice developing the skills that allow them to thrive in college-level online courses, colleges should pay special attention to online courses for first-year students.

What does the evidence say about online courses? It's mixed, depending on how well the course is run. It's certainly true that online courses can increase access to higher education for students who would otherwise not be able to take classes because of location or schedule restrictions. However, the challenge is that many online courses, particularly asynchronous courses, may fail to integrate the learner-centered teaching practices and student support discussed above. Researchers find that low-quality courses are especially characterized by a lack of "meaningful interaction among students and between students and faculty," which limits student learning and success (Protopsaltis & Baum, 2019, p. 1). As a result, many students, especially those from underrepresented and low-income backgrounds, often do worse in online courses than in in-person ones, with lower grades and higher dropout rates (Protopsaltis & Baum, 2019).

Some approaches to online course delivery have tried to address these shortcomings. A professor can structure the course to enable student learning, enhancing communication and providing meaningful instructor–student and student-to-student interaction. The same qualities that make an in-person course strong should be present in online courses as well; you'll want to find online courses with learner-centered approaches, translated to an online environment. These approaches to online education can, when done well, help develop strong student competencies and learning outcomes, as well as increasing student satisfaction with the course. As you consider different online courses, you should think carefully about whether the class is set up to facilitate student engagement and support, instead of exacerbating disparities.

ACADEMIC OFFERINGS AND MAJOR SELECTION

When students apply to college, they are typically asked to indicate a major. Majors are an area of concentration in which a student will take a series of courses to build some depth of understanding and skills in a subject, like history, or biology, or political science. Majors can also be interdisciplinary, in which they incorporate and bridge several fields to examine a focus area, like interdisciplinary social sciences where students take courses in a few concentration areas—say, economics, political science, and sociology—to build and bridge understanding from multiple perspectives.

There are so many majors in higher education today, and new ones are created by colleges each year. Selecting one can be hard, and students can feel tremendous pressure from many different directions. Some entering students feel that they ought to know already what they want to do and, when they don't have their minds made up, decide they are somehow inadequate. Other students do enter college convinced they know what they want to do; sometimes this gets in the way of their ability to consider other possibilities and change their course of study to one that turns out to be in better alignment with their talents and desires.

Carmen believed he would become a lawyer. When he entered college, he had his entire life plan set around that career goal. The only area of study he even considered was political science; he never so much as researched other programs at his college. Why would he? He thought he knew exactly how to get into law school. Spring of his first year, though, Carmen was required to take an elective course outside of his major. He decided to take a course in physics for non-majors. He was shocked to discover that he found the course material more engaging than that in all his other science classes, and he excelled on assignments and exams. He took another class, excelled again, and realized he had a deep interest in the subject. Ultimately, though, Carmen never changed his major from political science—he couldn't envision deviating from the life path he had charted for himself in high school.

Some in higher education refer to students like Carmen who hold this mindset as being "foreclosed" students; that is, the students' minds are not open to thinking about other opportunities or pathways. A "foreclosed" mind, however, may be misguided, since it can prevent students from considering ways that they can be challenged to grow, change, and experiment. It can also block students from reconsidering what path might be best aligned with their talents and interests.

For some, selecting a major is driven primarily by thinking about which degree path will land a good job soon after graduation or what will satisfy the expectations of others in their lives. There is also a societal push for students to pursue degrees in science, technology, math, and health professions, among others, positing that these lead to strong employment outcomes. Accordingly, students often align their selected major with specific job openings or median salaries. Many colleges, higher education websites, and even the federal government provide data concerning salaries and employment outcomes to help students make informed decisions about different majors.

Common wisdom will also tell students to reflect on what they like and want to do, and then to pick a major. After all, without an internally motivated interest and curiosity in a field, students tend not to perform well and find it hard to push through when challenges arise. But with a new college student's limited range of life experiences, it can be hard to know one's true interests and passions. When a student enters college, they may be unaware of the full range of different fields, careers, and problems that exist in the world. As a result, many will naturally gravitate to the professions that they have interacted with or admire, such as medicine, law, engineering, nursing, or business. But picking a major solely based on what a student has been exposed to may prevent them from learning about different areas of study.

It is reasonable to consider statistics on majors and their job outcomes when planning a course of study, but students should not focus exclusively on data about past performance. Technological and other changes drive changes in the labor market, and the job you prepare for today may not exist in a decade. The COVID-19 pandemic, for instance, illustrated how quickly the ways we operate and conduct business can be upended and reformed. To navigate this changing landscape, students can cultivate broad interests. They can also consider what problems in the world they are passionate about addressing and focus their skills development accordingly. How can students plan their major, courses, and engagement outside of the classroom to foster the core competencies they will need to be ready for life after graduation in a changing world?

Fortunately, selecting a major does not need to be done alone, nor does it have to happen by just thinking about what you want to do. Colleges can and should facilitate students' selection and provide guidance to students from a variety of sources, from advisors, alumni, employment data, professors, and more. Guidance should also be complemented by students engaging in a set of diverse experiences so that they can make an informed, purposeful decision.

Despite the anxiety around selecting the "right" major in college, a student's major does not define their life trajectory. While some may argue that only certain, practical majors lead to employment and a good life while others will not and are a "waste of time and money," that just does not match what happens to students (Brooks, 2012). As numerous studies and surveys from the American Association of Colleges and Universities (AAC&U) have found, employers endorse a broad college education, regardless of major, with diverse experiences and a focus on developing cross-cutting skills as the best preparation for long-term career and life success (Pasquerella, 2019).

According to the AAC&U, over 90% of employers believe that employees' capacity to think, communicate, and problem-solve is more important than their college major. Employers "place a premium" on employees' ability to innovate "in response to rapid change," and they favor those with broad educational experiences over narrow technical training (Pascarella, 2019). A good college major program will have courses that cultivate these skills, as well as allow for (or require) internships, service learning, international study, or other forms of experiential learning that are high impact and formative.

It is true that some professions may require or prefer a particular undergraduate or graduate degree to obtain a license to practice. But this is often not the case. A particular major is often not required for employment, and many companies will give specific training to their employees. In addition, research from the U.S. Federal Reserve has found that a small minority of people have a job that is directly related to their major (Abel & Deitz, 2016). Graduates are also likely to change careers or jobs (Coffey et al., 2019). While first jobs out of college tend to be more aligned with a student's major, by the third job, people tend to be doing something quite different. For STEM majors, research has found that people often start leaving STEM occupations after about a decade, perhaps once their skills are not as aligned with the latest needs or career ambitions evolve (Deming & Noray, 2019).

Research finds that students in many majors, even disciplines as different as humanities and technology, often end up in similar sorts of organizational functions in their career as they move up positions and occupy more management-oriented roles. It is true that starting salaries for graduates from certain disciplines like engineering or computer science may be higher than others, such as humanities. However, salaries tend to even out as people change jobs and advance in their careers (Coffey et al., 2019).

While there can be distinct benefits of majoring in a STEM program, it is important to consider what limitations might also arise, particularly for those programs that have a more narrow technical skills training focus. Since technology and labor markets change rapidly, it is critical for STEM majors to find academic programs and other experiences that cultivate in-depth training in communication, writing, and collaboration—the sorts of skills that are transferable across time and professional roles. In addition, careful attention should be given to a college's retention and graduation rates for students in their STEM programs. Research has found that underrepresented students, particularly students who are Black and Latinx, leave STEM programs at nearly twice the rate as their White counterparts (Riegle-Crumb et al., 2019). This is due to many reasons, including a lack of inclusive or learner-centered teaching approaches, as discussed above.

Regardless of a student's major, college is not the end of learning—there should be an expectation of lifelong and continuous learning. While students can prepare for their first job in college, they will also need to cultivate transferable skills, curiosity, and a learning mindset to help prepare for their third, fourth, and fifth jobs. Students can also go to graduate or professional school after college in a different field than the one they studied as undergraduates. A philosophy student, for example, can go into a Master's in Social Work program.

There are also robust lifelong learning opportunities provided by colleges, companies, and many other organizations that help people and employees evolve and develop new skills as the economy, technology, and labor markets change. Students should anticipate a future of continued growth, learning, and development.

DOUBLE MAJORS AND COMBINED BACHELOR'S + MASTER'S PROGRAMS

Students, especially those who earned college credits in high school, may elect to do a second major, also known as a double major, during college. Others may even pursue two simultaneous bachelor's degrees, also known as dual degrees. Pursuing a double major or dual degree is common among students who earned college course credits while still in high school, like Nara. She completed two majors, in philosophy and social sciences. The philosophy major, she reasoned, would give her a grounding in how the world ought to be, while the social science focus on policy would help her figure out how to make it so. These were complementary academic paths, allowing Nara to ask and try to answer big questions in the world.

While there isn't clear evidence to suggest that doing a double major inherently produces higher salaries or improves life outcomes after college, adding a second major may have a positive impact on students' learning and on returns on their investments in higher education. This is particularly true if the second major complements the skills of the first, such as adding a statistics major to a philosophy major. These returns are reduced if the second major results in significant delays to a student's graduation. This is why many colleges have policies that place limits to when students can declare a second major. For many colleges, a student must declare a double major no later than their junior year. If a student decides to pursue a second major when they are close to graduation, they will usually need to extend their time in college.

Many colleges offer bachelor's and master's combined pathways, in which students complete their bachelor's degree and master's degree in a shorter amount of time than if they were done separately. At DePaul University, for instance, students studying marketing can join their Combined Bachelor's and Master's Degree program (DePaul University, n.d.). Students can complete 12 credit hours of graduate courses while still undergraduates. The graduate credits count for both the bachelor's and master's degrees, allowing students to complete both on an expedited timeline of 5 years, rather than 5 1/2 or 6.

Students with college credit earned during high school may be good candidates for these programs. If a student arrives at college with a significant number of college credits, it may even be possible for them to complete both their bachelor's and master's degrees in 4 years. In this case, a student may complete a bachelor's in 3 years and a master's in the fourth year. In fact, some students may want to consider a master's degree rather than doing a double major as an undergraduate. Students with a master's degree can be more competitive in seeking employment or further graduate education, such as programs in law or medicine, or even a second master's or PhD. There are often implications for financial aid and other policies, however, that need to be understood before embarking on a double major or combined degree pathway.

WHAT ABOUT UNDECIDED MAJORS?

Recognizing that many students are not ready to declare a major at the start of college, most colleges have an undecided "major" that can be declared for the first year or two of college. (Undecided is also referred to as "exploratory" or "undeclared.") Certain colleges won't even allow students to declare a major until their second year.

Some students who are undecided may struggle to identify a major or career path that ignites their passions and motivates them to persist in higher education. Many colleges find that students who remain undecided through their second year have lower graduation rates than those who make a major selection (Venit, 2016). In light of this, some colleges help undecided students explore potential areas of study and career fields. These colleges provide specialized guidance to help students identify and declare a major. This may include helping a student select courses to sample different areas and connecting them with experiential learning opportunities, like job shadow and internship opportunities, to see if the students like a particular area or type of work. In addition, colleges, particularly community colleges, may also ask students to first select a meta-major instead of a specific major when they start. Meta-majors are typically broad areas, such as Social Sciences, Sciences, or Humanities. By picking a meta-major, students can start making progress toward their degree without having to commit to a specific area of study they still feel unsure about early in college.

LIMITED ACCESS AND RESTRICTED MAJORS

At many colleges, students apply to some specialized majors or programs through a competitive process for acceptance. These are often known as limited access programs, restricted majors, or limited enrollment majors. While some colleges admit students into their programs during the first year, other colleges require students to apply later, often during their second year. This means that just getting into the college does not guarantee acceptance into a specific major. A student may, for instance, need at least a 3.2 college GPA for the first 2 years of college to gain admission to the business major.

Colleges have these limited access programs for a few reasons. Certain majors have restricted capacity and high demand from students. Nursing is one such common example. Because students in nursing programs are usually required to complete clinical hours in the field, the number of students an undergraduate nursing program can accept is often limited by clinical sites in a community. Other programs, such as music performance, typically require a high level of mastery of a particular skill at the start of the major.

Some academic departments in colleges posit that having competitive admissions criteria for their majors is important to maintain standards and rigor. They may view the prerequisite courses for admission to a major as opportunities to identify the strongest students and to reduce the pool of candidates for admission. The challenge, however, is that when courses are designed as "weed-out" courses, the department is effectively designing the course to not promote the success of students; they may, instead, be anticipating that many of the students will fail the course. Complicating this dynamic is that weed-out courses may rely on less effective teaching models that don't sufficiently engage, challenge, and support the diversity of learners.

It's very possible, however, that if these courses were taught with more evidence-based approaches, students' performance could dramatically improve. But if there are too many competitive applicants for a major, colleges again face the same dilemma: What should the college do when they don't have enough spots for everyone who has applied?

After being rejected from limited access programs, students often have to figure out a whole new academic and career path. Some simply change majors and remain at the college, but others drop out or transfer to another institution to pursue their degree. This often creates financial and emotional complications for the student.

It is important to check with colleges on these kinds of limited access practices. A good starting point is to ask the college if they have limited access programs, and, if so, how competitive the application process is. In addition to the admissions requirements, you will want to know the graduation requirements too. You should also ask the college how they support students who do not get accepted into a limited access program: Does the college provide special advising and guidance for students so they can consider and map out alternative plans?

CHANGING MAJORS

Many students change majors during college. Data from the U.S. National Center for Education Statistics (NCES, 2017b) finds that about one-third of students change their major at least once, and about one out of 10 students changes majors two or more times.

While some people think that changing majors negatively affects students, this is not always the case. Changing majors can be positive. In fact, research has found that students who change majors up until their third year graduate at higher rates, on average, than those who stay in the same major their entire time in college (Venit, 2016). Why? Because changing majors indicates that a student is taking ownership of their learning and affirmatively realigning their academic path with their interests, goals, or aspirations.

However, changing majors multiple times, or very late in a college career (i.e., end of junior year or later), tends to reduce the chances of graduation for students or extend their time to graduation, as students will often end up needing to take additional courses to graduate. In fact, about 75% of students who change majors late in their college career do not graduate in 4 years, if at all (Venit, 2016).

EARNING COLLEGE CREDIT IN HIGH SCHOOL

Students may have different opportunities to earn college credit while in high school. Some high schools offer programs like Advanced Placement (AP), International Baccalaureate (IB), or Cambridge Advanced International Certificate of Education (AICE). Other high schools may allow students to dual-enroll, meaning that they can take college classes while still working to earn their high school diploma. Regardless of the route these students take, they arrive at college with college credits earned in high school. These can help students graduate in a timely manner, in 4 years or even less. Entering college with accelerated credits can also allow more flexibility in a student's program because they have already fulfilled some general education requirements.

But many students who have earned accelerated credits in high school still report wanting a 4-year college experience, even if they can finish earlier. As a result, many students choose to add a second major so that they have an academic pathway that will take 4 years to complete. However, the advanced credit can have implications, particularly if the student wants to spend 4 years as a full-time college student. Since these students can enter college with the first year or two of college credits already completed, they will often be asked by the college to declare a major immediately at matriculation and very soon after be pushed to enter major-specific courses alongside college juniors and seniors. There may also be implications for financial aid from the college, state, or federal government since students will accumulate many credit hours very quickly and approach financial aid limits which cap the number of hours a student can have earned toward a degree and still receive aid. Finally, the college may have policies that automatically graduate students once they complete the degree requirements, making it difficult to stay a full 4 years if you arrive with significant credit hours. Given these practices, prospective students should ask colleges to walk them through how these credits may impact their time at the college.

To accommodate students who have earned accelerated credit in high school and want to graduate efficiently, some colleges have developed structured programs that allow students to finish a bachelor's degree in 3 years or less, sometimes known as degree-in-three programs. These efforts aim to optimize a student's course schedule to complete the degree in 3 years, while also encouraging the student to engage in other important activities outside of classes that will prepare them to be successful after graduation.

WHAT STUDENTS CAN DO BEFORE COLLEGE TO PREPARE

Since many colleges ask applicants to indicate a major in their application or to officially declare it soon after arriving in college, students in high school may want to begin guided exploration of various academic paths, including career discussions and how they may want to impact the world. At a fundamental level, engaging in a wide variety of experiences in high school is helpful for students to make informed decisions in college about what they want to study and how they want to use their talents to contribute to the world.

But how does a high school student prepare for the rigor of a college curriculum? It's hard to fully prepare in advance, but students should get used to putting in the hard work in high school. By setting habits in which students put forth their best effort, they will be better prepared for the demands of a college course load. Students should hold a growth mindset, engaging with high school course material seriously, challenging themselves to develop new skills, and being an active learner in the classroom and beyond. Overall, high school students should aim to take a curriculum that is sufficiently challenging for them to develop while also engaging in enrichment opportunities in the school, such as clubs and community service, that provide a preparatory foundation for college success.

THREE GUIDING QUESTIONS TO ASK ABOUT THE CURRICULUM

1. To what extent does the college use evidence-based teaching practices, such as active learning, and how effective is the teaching in ensuring that all students learn?
2. To what extent does the college have clear, guided pathways of courses to completion, and do these curricular pathways build students' skills efficiently and effectively?
3. To what extent does the academic pathway exist for you to achieve your goals, and can you get the courses you need to graduate in a timely fashion?

Table 3.1. A Rubric for Evaluating a College's Curriculum

Level	Indicators
Excellent	Curriculum has articulated pathways and thoughtful learning outcomes at several stages and for each major; professors use research-based, learner-centered teaching practices; college has few disparities in course completion rates among its various demographic groups in the student body; college has enough course availability so students can progress without delay; excellent teaching is celebrated and rewarded.
Good	Guided pathways and appropriate learning outcomes are present through the curriculum; professors widely deploy learner-centered teaching practices; there are not widespread disparities in course completion rates; college has very limited occasions of insufficient course capacity to meet students' need to progress in a timely way.
Average	Learner-centered teaching practices are partially deployed across the curriculum, with some departments and majors not fully embracing or practicing them; there are gaps in course completion rates among the student body and regular occasions of insufficient course capacity.
Fair	Curriculum has stated learning objectives, but the college cannot or does not articulate how courses actually develop the learning outcomes; large course completion rate disparities exist and insufficient course capacity is common; teaching practices often do not incorporate learner-centered approaches.
Poor	Curriculum is poorly constructed without clear learning outcomes for students; instructors primarily use instructor-centered, lecture-based teaching approaches; substantial disparities in course completion rates exists, particularly in 1st- and 2nd-year courses; college offers insufficient course availability to meet student demand.

CHAPTER 4

Staying on Track
Academic and Student Support

Brianna was excited to start college, but anxious about what it entailed. Her first 100 days were filled with highs and lows: making new friends, exploring a new city, having her own dorm room, but also continually struggling with navigating an unfamiliar academic environment. One of the first obstacles arose even before she left home: choosing her courses. Both of her parents had attended the same college as Brianna. Brianna knew she wanted to study Creative Writing, while her parents wanted her to study Business. As she was selecting her courses for her first semester, she was frustrated by her parents' pressure to follow a schedule they'd picked out. Brianna compromised and selected a mix of courses.

But when she arrived at college, she found that even talking with professors after class stressed her out, much less going to visit them in their offices. Brianna remembers burning with embarrassment when she received her first exam grade in macroeconomics. It was 63%, much lower than she'd anticipated. In high school, her parents would help her study and review class material—but now that she was at college, Brianna wanted to be independent and develop her own ways of doing things. She decided to go to her college's tutoring center, swallowing her embarrassment around needing tutoring in the first place. When she arrived at the tutoring center, she found that there weren't any tutors available for her specific class; if she wanted help with macroeconomics, she would need to wait and come back another day. Brianna was frustrated at not being able to meet with a tutor, but even more frustrated at the thought of returning to the tutoring center without a guarantee of getting help.

A few weeks later, Brianna discovered that she needed to turn in a form to drop a course after the seventh week of the semester on the very day the form was due. She hadn't received an email alerting her of this due date; it was just something that she was expected to know. Instead of being delivered to the English Department, like her other paperwork, this form needed to go to the Dean's Office. Brianna didn't know where the Dean's Office was, and she was flustered as she rushed to fill out the paperwork, get the appropriate signatures, and find the right building. The difficulties in filling out and delivering that form exemplified the frustration and confusion Brianna often felt. As she navigated across her first 100 days, Brianna increasingly felt like college was a mystery, making her question if she could thrive there.

As Brianna's story shows, every step of the college journey can present new challenges and choices about unfamiliar topics that many students don't know how to navigate. Some students don't know what opportunities even exist. It is easy for students to feel like college is a place where they don't belong, particularly for students who are the first generation in their families to attend. Without experience in college, how would you know that going to a specific series of events on campus would be important, or when (or if) to schedule a meeting with a career advisor, or how to start engaging in research with a professor, or how to build an optimal course schedule?

Research in higher education demonstrates that constructive guidance, structure, and programming can help make significant differences in students' abilities to navigate higher education, to make productive decisions, and to feel that they belong and are important to the college. Colleges have come a long way in this regard. For many years, students were mostly left on their own to try and navigate through college. Without many constraints imposed by the institution, students searched for resources and picked their courses from a catalog, without any outside input, save the rare meeting with a professor or by asking friends and family for advice. The "support" students received from the college generally took a reactive approach, in which students were expected to reach out when they had problems and questions. These colleges had expectations of a certain level of agency and understanding among students: When students wanted or needed something, they would make themselves known.

Over time, and as college-going populations became larger and more diverse, higher education began to see the shortcomings of this approach. Colleges saw that students often failed to ask for help, or asked for help too late, and they ended up doing poorly or leaving college altogether. Many students reported that they didn't feel connected to and supported by their colleges. Some say that lacking a sense of belonging was a principal reason why they left college entirely.

Colleges started to realize that students needed different kinds of support, at different times. They saw that this support needed to be customized to students' needs and delivered more proactively, coordinated by trained professionals. Student success practices at many colleges now recognize the diversity of students they have, use data to identify risk factors that suggest a student may need assistance, and build the right sets of support, outreach, and engagement to help students succeed and grow.

Critics argue that colleges who deploy these kinds of efforts are just coddling students, and that we should let students figure it out on their own; after all, when they graduate, employers are not going to "coddle" their employees in this way, right (Yi, 2016)? Similarly, some critics suggest that admission to college should solely be viewed as an opportunity. In this view, admission to college is simply giving students the chance to prove that they have what it takes to succeed and to show what they are capable of doing. Accordingly, colleges don't have a responsibility to help their students thrive.

One key problem with this line of reasoning is that it assumes an equal playing field for all students. Colleges are now much more complex and diverse, and students come to college with many different perspectives and backgrounds. When many systems and programs in colleges were designed and implemented, a wide breadth of student backgrounds was not considered. As student bodies have grown more diverse, many of these systems have failed to adapt, if they even existed in the first place. Why would we expect someone to know how to start college and navigate a new and foreign environment in an optimal way?

Colleges ask students to understand how to be a good student from the time they begin their academic careers. Many colleges assume that students will already know how to communicate with a faculty member, what sorts of things are important to do, and when to go to a professor's office hours, for example. However, for students that have limited familiarity with the intricacies of college, this maze of requirements and expectations acts as a sort of hidden curriculum, often hindering students' ability to thrive and feel like they belong. And when students don't feel that they belong, that they are supported by the college, they tend to have lower academic performance, graduation rates, and increased rates of stress and mental health challenges (Gopalan & Brady, 2019). Higher education professionals now know the extent of damage that colleges that are poorly designed and structured can have on students, especially for first-generation college students.

Today, much more is known about how students develop, and what works in student advising, services, and support. Designing the college experience to engage, challenge, and support students, and providing sustained and substantive relationships with advisors and professionals can make a huge difference (Mayhew et al., 2016). These advisors and mentors can offer guidance to help demystify higher education and its many, often opaque requirements. They can help students make good decisions and develop positive habits and behaviors, as well as new skills in professionalism and time management. They can help students feel supported and that they belong there, so that students are more able to explore and to challenge and push themselves through obstacles. They can advocate for students, introduce them to other professionals on campus, and guide them into new growth opportunities. These professionals recognize that college students are transitioning from more structured environments of high school to less structured environments of college, as students' identities evolve and they learn to exercise new forms of agency.

This hardly seems like coddling. Students still have to make choices and encounter difficulties. Even with support from a college, students will still be challenged inside and outside the classroom. Well-designed courses, projects, internships, presentations, essays, and even conversations with peers will push students and propel their growth. And no matter what colleges do, students may still encounter difficulties in their lives, many of which reflect broader societal obstacles: challenges in their home life; cultural assimilation; family interactions with the criminal justice system; food and housing insecurity; racism; mental health struggles; and many others. Some students will have to balance academics with working multiple jobs, caring for dependents, or both. These social and environmental contexts for a student can shape how they view themselves and their place in college, but they can also present real and pressing obstacles that hinder students' ability to complete the many tasks of higher education.

In order to foster student success, many colleges have invested in developing a robust network of ways for students to be supported and engaged. As we will explore in this chapter, this can include advising, life coaching, tutoring and supplemental instruction, libraries, orientation, first-year success programs, and much more.

ADVISING AND MENTORING

Advisors and mentors play a central role in helping students thrive in higher education. Advisors and mentors can help students feel connected to the institution, navigate academic and institutional challenges, and connect to resources and opportunities. Research shows that advisors, particularly high-quality ones, can significantly increase students' performance and graduation rates (Canaan et al., 2019).

In the narrow view, advisors are there to help students ensure their completion of their degree. They help students select and plan courses; provide guidance on learning strategies and study skills; connect students to college resources, such as financial aid, tutoring, and counseling; and identify and overcome institutional and personal barriers that can hinder students' progress to graduation.

But advisors, particularly at colleges with robust student success ecosystems and where advising is intentional and integrated into the student experience, do even more than merely ensure students obtain their degree. As we will explore below, there are many types of advising and mentorship outside of academics. Advisors deal with a range of questions, such as: What should I major in? What should I do after I graduate? I don't feel like I belong here; what do I do? What else should I be doing in college beyond courses? I'm not making friends, what should I do?

Excellent advisors view students holistically, using a developmental approach to help students understand their educational potential. They help students have the right sets of experiences not only to make progress toward their degree, but also to engage and challenge themselves to thrive in college and realize their best selves. They help students build skills, make good decisions about financing college, balance academic and nonacademic obligations (e.g., taking care of a family member, work, and so forth), and overcome other personal or academic obstacles. Advisors help students create balance and manage stress, boost students' self-confidence, and formulate goals.

High-quality advisors notice when things are going wrong with a student, when there is a break in a pattern of behavior—and they try to help address students' problems before they escalate. In other words, these advisors are proactive. They listen to students' concerns and questions, inform students of important deadlines, and help students understand and navigate academic rules and policies. These advisors help students who are making their way in the world discern their talents and develop plans for life after graduation that align with them.

Great advising and mentoring also challenges students to engage in reflection and pursue new educational opportunities, pushing students to think deeply about themselves. It is easy for students to have fun in college, going about their days and staying busy. But it's important for students to take time along the way to reflect, and advisors and others can prompt a student's introspection. They can help students reflect on behavior and form positive habits, empowering students to find their own solutions to challenges. Advisors can push students to ask questions about how they could have done things differently or how they can use the resources of the college and beyond to get through a situation.

In short, advisors help students in forming and achieving personal, academic, and professional goals. Doing this well requires a college to have enough advisors for all the students when they need them, not just the select few who may regularly make their way to their advisor.

Recognizing the benefits of advising, many colleges require students to meet with an advisor as part of a mandatory process. Students may be required to visit their academic advisor each semester or term to ensure they are on track in their academic plans and to discuss their overall experience. Mandatory advising practices can be helpful for students, particularly in the first year and for students who would otherwise think that they do not need to consult with anyone. When students solely rely on themselves for advising (self-advising) they may be prone to costly errors or misunderstandings that unnecessarily extend their time in college, signing up for the wrong classes or missing important academic milestones, for instance. They may also miss out on learning about opportunities, resources, or the benefits of mentorship and professional guidance.

Take Crystal. She had rarely needed her high school guidance counselors, so she didn't see the point in talking to her college academic advisors. As a dietetics major, Crystal knew she needed to take a counseling course called Foundations of Counseling—but she didn't realize that she needed to take it by the end of her third semester in order to be prepared for other key classes. Crystal discovered her oversight too late and had to take the class the following semester. As a result, she had to delay taking the classes that required having passed Foundations of Counseling, and her progress toward a timely graduation was impeded.

FORMS OF ADVISING AND MENTORING

There are various types of advising and mentoring that extend across nearly all areas of college life. Many student-success colleges now have all of these kinds of advisors and supporters working in concert with one another to meet the diverse needs of students in higher education.

Faculty: Faculty, instructors at a college, can serve as formal advisors for students, particularly at smaller colleges or in academic departments/majors without many students. Faculty can also serve as mentors to provide broader life and career guidance to students.

Professional Academic Advisors: Professional academic advisors are the paid staff of the college who help students select majors, build course schedules, stay engaged, and more. Advisors can specialize in certain populations or majors, such as transfer students or engineering students. Some colleges also use trained peer advisors (fellow students) to supplement professional advising.

Life Coaching: College Life Coaches, also known as Success Coaches, are paid staff who work with students to establish goals—both academic and non-academic—and help students reach them. Life coaches tend to work more holistically and intensively than professional academic advisors. It's not uncommon for a student to meet with their life coach every 2 weeks. (Staff at some colleges blend the role of professional advisors and life coaches.)

Fellowship/Scholarship Advisors: These advisors are paid staff who help students interested in applying for competitive scholarships, fellowships, and awards, such as the Rhodes, Fulbright, and Truman scholarships. Often, these awards help pay for college or graduate school and bring recipients together for special programming. Advisors will help students determine which fellowships or scholarships are within a student's interest, and help students plan and apply for them. A student may go to a fellowship advisor for assistance in reflecting on their experiences, refining application materials, or drafting a personal statement.

Mentors: Mentoring programs often involve pairings of a more experienced person, such as an upper-level student, staff, or community member, and a student. Typically, there is special training involved for mentors, and the relationship can help provide information, support, and guidance along a number of issues. Mentors can help students with interpersonal skills and career development, as well as with troubleshooting academic or life problems (Mayhew et al., 2016). While a college may have formal mentorship programs, mentorship relationships can also form organically as students move through higher education.

Using data from a national survey of alumni, researchers have found that having a constellation of many mentors amplifies how satisfied college graduates are with their education. The research recommends that students build a "diverse set of faculty, staff and peers who will get students out of their comfort zones and challenge them to learn more—and more deeply—than they thought they could" (Lambert et al., 2018). Students with a diverse set of mentors are more likely to report their college experience as very rewarding, especially compared to students who had no such relationships. Peer relationships also positively impact students' college experience. Research indicates that students should start building their mentorship network as early as possible.

Given the importance of advising and mentoring, students should assess what each college offers. Some colleges may have publicly displayed information about their advising and mentoring structure and resources, but many will not. You can also check websites and ask questions of the college about what kind of advisors and mentors they have at the institution and their approaches to working with students. One of the basic things you'll want to know is a college's student-to-advisor ratio and how it varies across campus. While you may be able to surface this information by digging through a college's website, the simplest way to find out is to ask the college admissions office directly what the ratio is and how it is distributed. There may be uneven levels of support: In one department, such as Fine Arts, it may be one advisor for every 100 students, but for another department, like Business, it may be one advisor for every 1,000 students. Especially when the ratio is extreme, there may be little consistency in which advisor a student sees. A student might meet with a different person every time they go to advising, making it difficult to build relationships or ensure accuracy of information. While there are differing perceptions on what ratio is optimal, many recommend that there be no more than 300 students for every advisor in the college (Moody, 2019). Ideally, the ratio should be even lower, particularly among life coaching. By learning about the student-to-advisor ratio, prospective students can broadly gauge to what extent students may have access to advisors.

Students would also want to assess a college's approach to mentorship: What programs or structured opportunities are there for mentorship from peers, alumni, faculty, and others? While many of these relationships have the capacity to form organically, without encouragement and structure students may struggle to form and develop connections. In fact, national survey data of college graduates suggests that less than half had a mentor during college who "encouraged them to pursue their goals and dreams" (Strada-Gallup, 2018, p. 4).

SUPPORT FOR UNDERREPRESENTED AND UNDERSERVED STUDENTS

Many students who start college do not graduate. Unfortunately, many of the students who leave without a degree are students who are historically underrepresented or underserved. Students attending higher education are incredibly diverse and include a variety of underrepresented groups: students who are veterans, LGBTQ+, experiencing homelessness, disabled, Black, Latinx, the first in their family to attend college, from a rural area, have dependents, and more.

Students from a variety of marginalized backgrounds attend higher education at lower rates, and they disproportionately do not persist in higher education. Many colleges use data to identify why certain students are not staying or doing well in their college, and then launch programs to address challenges, remove barriers, engage students, build community, and ameliorate disparities. Some colleges have erased these disparities entirely.

Not all students need the same approach toward thriving in higher education. Some colleges use programs with a lighter touch, providing shared communities for students, or a resource center for students to gather, get support, and have activities. The most celebrated of programs that support student subpopulations, particularly for lower-income student populations, include comprehensive services that can last from admission through to graduation. They can provide funding, even covering housing and food costs, build community, set high expectations, connect students to support and out-of-class engagement opportunities such as internships and research, and help hold students accountable as they progress. Some of these programs also help students balance their educational needs with the needs of their family (Escarcha, 2019). Done well, participating in these programs is a point of pride for students, fostering a sense of belonging at the college.

There are many excellent examples of programs to support targeted student populations at colleges around the country. Award-winning programs include the Accelerated Study in Associate Programs (ASAP) at the City University of New York, which supports lower-income students and provides public transportation passes, specialized advising and support, financial aid, and more (Strumbos et al., 2018). Another program, the Center for Academic Retention and Enhancement (CARE) at Florida State University, provides a 4-year experience, starting in the summer before the first year of college, for students who are both low-income and the first generation in their families to attend college (Klopfenstein, 2019).

The CARE program cohorts students and is relatively structured in the beginning. It includes sets of common experiences and classes, tutoring, mandatory study sessions, college life coaching, academic advising, peer mentoring, career advising, required workshops and attendance at some campus-wide activities and events, options for study abroad, internships, and more. As the students in the program learn and practice how to be successful college students in the first year, building skills and positive habits, the requirements of the program relax and students are empowered to navigate higher education and allocate their time without as much program structure.

Several California State University campuses, such as Northridge and San Marcos, have award-winning programs to support students who are Latinx (Excelencia in Education, n.d.). These colleges take varying approaches that provide learning communities and shared experiences for students, including dedicated advising from both peers and professionals, common courses taken as a cohort in which Latinx identity is discussed and taught by Latinx professors, and community service and campus activities.

In an effort to lift student success, especially for those from underrepresented backgrounds or are underrepresented in a certain subject, many colleges have bridge programs that ask students to start college early (e.g., in the summer) and move through intensive support and engagement programs. These can be academic major or subject focused, such as a math summer bridge to elevate math preparedness for college, or more general bridge programs, which help students transition to college and build community so they are more likely to do well once the academic year is fully started.

The NevadaFIT program at the University of Nevada, Reno, for example, offers a weeklong intensive bootcamp to prepare students for college. The participating students do college-level work and assignments, and they receive feedback from faculty. This allows students to fail "in a low-stakes environment," which helps the students build academic perseverance (Escarcha, 2019). The students also receive mentorship from peers who offer guidance on being a college student and the resources available to them. The peer mentors then check in on the students throughout the first semester. Some bridge programs continue throughout the year, or even across the 4 years of college. Done well, the bridge programs can lift student success rates in courses and at the college generally, including elevating student performance and reducing disparities among underrepresented students.

Colleges should also have robust academic services specifically for students with disabilities, such as students who are sight- or hearing-impaired, or paralyzed, as well as students who have less visible disabilities, such as dyslexia, bipolar disorder, autism, anxiety disorders, or depression. These students may need special testing accommodations in their classes, such as longer times for tests or a limited-distraction environment, notes taken for them by a fellow student during class, mobility assistance to navigate campus and get to classes, or materials in alternative formats like braille. College websites and instructional materials should be universally designed and accessible for students and others with disabilities. Overall, the culture of a college should be inclusive toward the diversity of students with disabilities and enable them to thrive.

The College Support Program (CSP) at Rutgers University is an example of a comprehensive support program for students with autism. CSP provides students with help defining their academic and professional goals, mentorship from peers and professional staff, life skills management (such as banking, hygiene, and household duties), career development, counseling, academic course support, and more (CSP, n.d.). CSP coordinates closely with partners across the campus, such as disability services, campus housing, career services, and faculty.

SUPPORT DURING EMERGENCY, NON-ACADEMIC LIFE EVENTS

College students, like all of us, have emergencies in their lives or changing circumstances that can create unexpected or sudden obstacles. A student may get in a car accident, develop a debilitating illness, or be a victim of a serious crime. Colleges should thus have robust medical, case management, and aid services. These services can help students navigate their difficulties. Many colleges have case management offices, which broadly exist to help students navigate extenuating circumstances in their lives. Case management, for instance, can help a student temporarily withdraw from the college for medical reasons and communicate with faculty. They also assist students in understanding college policies and procedures, working with financial aid, students' residential halls, and much more.

Take, for example, Trevor. He was from Florida, but attended college out of state, thousands of miles away. October of his sophomore year, a hurricane hit his hometown. His childhood house took heavy damages. Trevor recalled the shock of seeing his town on national news as reporters covered the aftermath of the storm. In the days following the storm, Trevor knew his family needed his help. His college, which centered student success, provided multiple avenues of response to the hurricane. Firstly, case managers assisted students like Trevor with communicating with professors and handling administrative forms associated with taking a longer absence from classes. Moreover, the college provided financial aid with Trevor's flight home, allowing him to travel easily. Members of the student body also rallied around Trevor and others affected, holding a food drive and fundraising for hurricane relief. The support from his college, and particularly from case management, was essential in Trevor responding well to a stressful situation entirely outside of his control.

PARENTAL AND FAMILY SUPPORT AND ENGAGEMENT

Families can play an important role in students' college journeys, particularly for young adults who, after all, make up the majority of the college-going population. For many students, college is seen as a journey for the whole family, not just the student alone. However, it is important to note the diversity of family backgrounds of college students. Not all students have a traditional two- or one-parent family structure, and older students may already have a more adult relationship with their parents. The relationship a student has with their guardian is often complex.

That said, for traditional populations, college brings new forms of independence and decisionmaking. Accordingly, attending college can change the parent–child relationship. In fact, national surveys and research indicates that it can strengthen bonds and improve relationships (College Pulse, 2019; Köber & Habermas, 2017). As students grow and mature into emerging adults, including taking on new adult responsibilities and managing life on their own, they tend to develop more and different understandings of their parents. Students tend to shift away from viewing parents merely as parents and toward seeing them as complex individuals. In doing so, students often come to view their parents less as authoritarians and more as peers who serve as confidants and advisors (Arnett, 2004; Birditt et al., 2008). It isn't a surprise, then, that research has found that parents, family, and close friends are students' primary sources of guidance and advice through college.

However, there are some challenges associated with going to parents and guardians for advice. While families can be important allies in the college process, providing motivation and boosting self-confidence, they also have the capacity to hinder students' growth and development.

Much research has found that a primary source of advice about financial aid is a students' parents, but that parents are often not familiar enough with the complexities of the financial aid procedures to provide accurate guidance (Long, 2008). Students also often ask their families about which courses they should take or major they should pursue. Families may not have the training or information to adequately sort through all the options, or they may not know the college's rules or requirements enough to give helpful and accurate advice. This may be especially the case with students who are the first generation in their families to attend college; researchers have found that they receive less financial and college-specific support from their parents than their peers whose parents attended college. Maietta (2016) describes a challenge associated with parents who have not attended college themselves navigating how to support their children:

> Parents often want to be involved, but are not sure what level of involvement is appropriate and what advice to provide. Some of these barriers are consistent with legacy [non–first generation] students as well, but these students often have a knowledgeable internal compass and external support system to help them navigate college. A fragile or non-existent support system layers stress and uncertainty to the college trajectory in general, and traverses the career planning process in particular. (para 7)

When students report feeling that their parents are over-involved, it can undermine the student's sense of self-confidence and agency, and decrease their psychological well-being (Schiffrin et al., 2013), an area we will discuss later in the book. While it's tempting for parents to help their student through every challenge, they should understand that too much assistance can actually undermine their child's development over the long term. Overparenting can even affect students in the workplace after graduation. Research has found that students who report overparenting expressed some maladaptive responses to challenges in the workplace and were less likely to take responsibility for themselves in situations where they experienced adversity (Bradley-Geist & Olson-Buchanan, 2014).

Colleges have sought to help students discuss boundaries and expectations with their families, and some have directly embraced the special role that families can have in helping students stay motivated and on track to graduate. The colleges most strongly geared toward student success recognize the important role families may play in students' lives, particularly for underrepresented students, and make efforts to include and educate them about the college journey and educational opportunities. Colleges may seek to educate parents and guardians about what types of opportunities their children should be engaged in, such as internships, so that parents can offer full and accurate advice. Colleges have also brought parents into their community through a variety of means: special orientation sessions, regular newsletters and communications, family and parent associations, and more.

More broadly, colleges should strive to use plain language that would be easily understood by students and families alike. As we discussed at the beginning of this chapter, college can seem like a mystery to many students, and highly technical, complex language contributes to anxiety and confusion. For many parents and guardians, this complicated language impedes their ability to support their children, as they too are confused. Unclear language coupled with byzantine bureaucracy may leave students overwhelmed and uncertain of their place at college, which resources to pursue, or how to succeed.

Some student success–oriented colleges conduct communication audits on themselves, looking across their communications with students, offices, websites, and forms to ensure that the language is presented in an accessible form for students and families. Many also translate materials into several languages, such as Spanish and Mandarin, for students and their family members to understand, as well as provide a "glossary of academic terms and acronyms that might be unfamiliar to most new students," as the University of Georgia has done for its new student handbook (Johnston, 2019). As you are looking at colleges, notice and evaluate the language they use in their publications to judge the ease with which a student may be able to navigate the administrative and bureaucratic aspects of a college.

STUDENT ENGAGEMENT WITH FACULTY

For many students, engaging with professors is intimidating and scary. Students may feel like imposters, anxious that they will be told they don't belong at the college or in a course. If students are already struggling or confused, the anxiety of going to a professor can be heightened. Students often ask themselves: Why would the professor want to talk with me? What do I have to offer? What will the professor think of me? What if I say the wrong thing? If I mess up, will the professor write a letter of recommendation for me?

Some of these questions were running through Addison's mind when she met with a professor outside of class for the first time in her sophomore year. Addison hadn't found her first-year classes too challenging; she had passed them easily, and without much studying. Her classes during her second year, though, were harder. Things just weren't clicking like they had in high school, or even last year. Her friends encouraged her to go to her professor, but she was resistant. She hadn't needed help before and thought of herself as being self-reliant. As her grade suffered, though, Addison realized she needed help. She remembers waiting anxiously in the hallway outside her professor's office, practicing what she would say. When Addison sat down with her professor, she was surprised to find the environment welcoming and easy-going. Addison explained what she was struggling with, and the professor worked through the first set of problems from the assignment with her. Instead of feeling anxious and out of place, Addison felt reassured and more confident in her ability to succeed in the class moving forward.

As Addison's case highlights and research shows, positive student–faculty interaction and mentorship can be hugely important for students. Even in the early days of higher education research, Astin (1977) found that "student–faculty interaction has a stronger relationship to student satisfaction with the college experience than any other student involvement variable." Chickering and Gamson (1991) found powerful effects on amplifying student motivation and involvement; they write, "Faculty concern helps students get through rough times and keep on working. Knowing a few faculty members well enhances students' intellectual commitment and encourages them to think about their own values and future plans" (p. 3). In other words, faculty–student engagement can bolster student learning and development, fostering both personal and intellectual growth (Padgett et al., 2012).

Student engagement with faculty can also hold implications for life after college. Research from the Gallup-Purdue Index, a college alumni survey, suggests that having a mentor in college who "encouraged your goals and dreams" is highly correlated to "success in work and life for college graduates," more than doubling a "graduate's odds of being engaged in their work and thriving in their overall well-being" (Busteed, 2019). Faculty mentors can promote long-term satisfaction across a variety of domains; they promote deep intellectual development during college, give guidance, and make connections that can launch students into graduate schools or careers. Unfortunately, the students who most need the extra time and interaction with professors are the least likely to seek them out.

One very common venue for this kind of interaction occurs in what professors call office hours. What are office hours? At a basic level, office hours are times outside of class at which the faculty member is scheduled to be available to engage with, offer guidance to, and answer questions from students. Many students are apprehensive about attending office hours. They report feeling anxious about knowing (or not knowing) what to say, asking for references, or feeling like they would be wasting the professor's time. Anthony Jack, a professor at the Harvard Graduate School of Education, helps reframe professor's office hours as opportunities for students to get to know faculty, be mentored, learn about the professor's experiences and research interests, and be connected to their professional networks (Nadworny, 2019).

Professors should explain to students what office hours are, when they are, and how they can be used, and encourage students to attend them. Faculty may hold office hours in various ways. As the name suggests, faculty commonly hold their office hours in their regular office. To make them more accessible and less intimidating, they may also hold them in a central, neutral site, like the library, coffee shop, residence hall, or a study lounge. They may also offer them virtually in video or phone sessions, and some in the evening to support students who are commuting or who work during the day. Some faculty even require students to visit their office hours early in the semester, or if they have larger classes, to come in groups, both of which can help alleviate fear and barriers that often prevent students from visiting office hours in the first place (Freishtat, 2020).

Building relationships with faculty members is key, particularly since graduate schools, fellowships, scholarships, and employers often require students to provide letters of recommendation. Some national fellowships, like the Rhodes Scholarship, ask that students get up to eight letters of recommendation. Eight! Without meaningful engagement and relationships with faculty members, it becomes very difficult for a student to procure substantive letters of recommendation, full of examples that illustrate important qualities about the student.

One important note for students to keep in mind is that professors are educators; they chose to go into higher education to work in an educational environment, which means they wanted, at some level, to work with students. Granted, the degree and ability of faculty members to work effectively with students varies considerably, but there is at least a common expectation that they should help students learn and grow, and office hours can be an important component in that process. Fundamentally, hosting office hours and engaging with students during them is part of a faculty member's job.

ACADEMIC SUPPORT: LIBRARIES, TUTORING, AND STUDY SKILLS

When people think of libraries, they often imagine not much more than stacks of books. College libraries, however, are much more than that. They play an important role in higher education. In addition to providing access to research and scholarly materials, college libraries also have specialized staff. These librarians can provide individualized support and skill building for students in locating and analyzing materials for their projects, particularly when doing undergraduate research and other projects that require analysis of research. Libraries also function as gathering and study spaces for students. At many colleges, libraries are a primary space for collaborative work. They are essential in facilitating the kind of academic community and collaborative environment that fosters student development and success.

Tutoring and supplemental instruction are also important to student success. Tutoring, done individually or in small groups by trained peer or professional tutors, can lift students' academic performance (Pascarella & Terenzini, 2005). Colleges that invest in student success offer widespread and targeted tutoring, integrated into many courses, particularly the courses that may present the most challenges for successful completion. The tutoring is accessible, typically without additional costs for students, and offered, in person or online, at times that students want and will use. While tutoring can be complementary to a course, it cannot replace excellent instruction like the kind we described in Chapter 3.

Study skill development is also important, since many students enter college without knowing how to study well. Maybe they were high achieving in high school and were able to absorb enough information to ace a test on their first try. Or maybe they just didn't have the time or motivation to study while they were in high school; they were busy working part-time jobs. Or they find that the type of studying they did in high school, staying up late to memorize flashcards, is insufficient for the rigor of their college courses. When students think of learning as just memorizing material and content, they tend not to have a good repertoire of study strategies because they don't understand that learning is much more than content—it's about developing reasoning skills and the ability to solve problems and work through novel situations. For many of these students, colleges can offer tutoring, specialized workshops, individual consultations, or in-class resources, which can be essential to giving students skills and strategies to study effectively and develop their reasoning.

SUPPORT DURING THE FIRST YEAR: ORIENTATION, ONBOARDING, AND TRANSITIONS

Orientation programs are when new students learn about the institution, typically get registered for courses with the help of an advisor, and start building community with other students and affinity toward the college. These are often done through in-person sessions over the course of 1 or 2 days in the summer before the students start at the college. But they can also include longer experiences that are more active, such as the Fish Camp at Texas A&M University (www.fish-camp.tamu.edu); be conducted online; or include a combination of these experiences. Unfortunately, some colleges do not even have an orientation session, or hold it for some, but not all, students—like students who are transferring to the institution or those who are attending an online program. Because orientations are often students' first substantive engagement on campus or with a college, it is important that these are done well, helping to establish a positive trajectory and a sense of belonging and connection.

When students complete orientation, they should have the information and perspectives they need to do well as they transition to college and start classes. Higher education is a labyrinth for many students, and the first semester is a critical time in which students engage with the college—or leave college altogether. Insufficient orientation and onboarding support will leave students struggling as they start college, compounding challenges for those already at risk of leaving higher education, such as lower-income students.

But orientation itself isn't sufficient to transition students into higher education, and strong student-success colleges have robust first-year programming that helps students adjust to their new environment. First-year programming teaches students how to access resources, such as tutoring, and connects them to career advising and counseling services. These programs build on the sense of belonging fostered by orientation and continue to integrate and build a college community. The programming can begin with welcoming activities in the first weeks of the semester and events that build connections, such as the Welcome to Michigan program at the University of Michigan (http://www.onsp. umich.edu/welcome-week). Some programs also familiarize students with the city or town in which the college is located.

Longer-term first-year student programming is often anchored in what is referred to as the "first year experience." This can take the form of first-year seminars, peer learning communities, informal discussion-based programming led by a more senior student, and so on. These intensive structures support the students' transition to a college. While there is significant variation in the form and content, generally these first-year experience efforts and courses are designed to help students continue to make friends, as well as introduce students to "campus resources, time management, study skills, career planning, cultural diversity, and student development issues" (Barefoot & Fidler, 1992, p. 2). These courses are typically taught by faculty, academic advisors, or student support staff, and they often include a peer leader (Upcraft et al., 2005), such as the University 101 courses at the University of South Carolina (https://sc.edu/about/offices_and_divisions/ university_101/index.php). Many of these first-year experience programs also bundle several connected or linked courses together as part of their regular curriculum, helping students build a community early on. Some programs, such as the Exploration Plan Program at Kent State University (www.kent.edu/exploratory) integrate opportunities for engaging in the community and volunteering, helping students connect and gain real-life application of course content.

Colleges have also realized that transitions occur at several points in a student's journey, and some colleges have "sophomore year experience" programming to support the new questions and challenges that arise as students progress and approach their more major-specific courses in their final years of college. Some colleges have extended this to develop structured programming for every year of college through to degree completion. Done well, these help students continuously take advantage of resources and opportunities for growth at each stage of their college journey.

WHAT STUDENTS CAN DO BEFORE COLLEGE TO PREPARE

One of the barriers to student success is knowing how to manage time and prioritize responsibilities, particularly as students adjust to college their first year. While there are many resources at a college to address this, students can prepare for the transition before beginning their college career. One helpful strategy before college and in each semester during college is to map out a learning schedule, a weekly schedule where students write down on a detailed calendar the activities and courses, including time for studying and out-of-class work, as well as time for meals and exercise and socializing for each day and at what times. This kind of learning schedule helps students manage their time and address the anxiety of being disorganized, which can also help them manage their academic stress during college (Struthers et al., 2000).

Students can also engage in academic conversations with their high school teachers so interaction with their faculty and instructors in college may be less intimidating (Padgett et al., 2012). Students can cultivate their support networks, the people and mentors who can help support and guide them as they transition into college. Just as college students should be engaged in self-reflection, as discussed earlier, so too should high school students. It may be particularly helpful for high school students to reflect on their strengths and interests, and when they should be proactive about reaching out to their support networks.

THREE GUIDING QUESTIONS TO ASK ABOUT ACADEMIC AND STUDENT SUPPORT

1. To what extent does the college have a system of high-quality advisors and mentors who work proactively with students and build relationships to advance student growth and progression?
2. To what extent does the college have appropriate resources, opportunities, and guidance to help students take advantage of learning opportunities in college and build community?
3. To what extent does the college have effective academic support programs for the full range of its students, including those for underrepresented populations?

Table 4.1. A Rubric for Evaluating a College's Academic and Student Support

Level	Indicators
Excellent	College has proactive, holistic, and effective academic advising, mentoring, and student support; sufficient staff exists to meet students' diverse needs and guide them to their full development; robust onboarding and transition support is present; college has substantial emergency assistance for students
Good	College provides advising, mentoring, and student support to address most student needs through a proactive approach, guiding students toward their full development; targeted programming is present, but it may let some students fall through the cracks unnoticed
Average	College provides advisors and other staff who aim to conduct more holistic advising, mentorship, and support, but there are not enough resources to reach all students; the quality of services is also inconsistent; student transition and onboarding efforts exist, with some tailoring to students' needs and diverse populations, but there are gaps
Fair	College provides advisors who generally have a limited focus on course registration, but not other areas of student support, with uneven levels of quality; limited programming, mentorship, and support services for students exist, focusing on some of the most at-risk student populations or special needs
Poor	College provides advisors who are not proactive and have an almost exclusive focus on course registration, with uneven levels of quality and far too few staff to meet student demand; college has very little student academic and community support programs, onboarding, or mentorship, even for students most at risk of attrition

Part III

DEVELOPING FULLY

CHAPTER 5

Beyond the Classroom
Applied and Experiential Learning

During Jonah's sophomore year, he decided he wanted to learn more about the legal profession, thinking that he would go to law school after graduation. He went onto his college's website, which listed a job shadowing program. He applied and was excited to be accepted. After informal interviews, Jonah spent a few days shadowing a defense attorney in his city. As the job shadowing position ended, Jonah asked if he could stay in touch during winter break. During the next couple of weeks, he continued to exchange emails with the attorney. At the beginning of the spring semester, Jonah was offered an internship position. He was elated to accept and excited to be gaining experience in the working world.

Jonah soon found that the internship was improving his abilities in the classroom too. In his communications class, he was able to connect readings from his textbooks to his experiences in the office. He had seen lawyers from the office use the rhetorical techniques outlined in the readings. Moreover, Jonah increasingly saw connections between his learning in the classroom and his internship, which made him more excited to learn. Class, which had sometimes felt boring or pointless, now seemed exciting and more relevant than ever. Learning how to communicate with different attorneys and other colleagues helped Jonah develop the confidence to reach out to his professors and to represent himself professionally, inside and outside academic spaces.

Jonah's job shadowing and internship speak to the transformative power of these out-of-class experiences. In 2005, researchers at the Center for Postsecondary Research at Indiana University set out to understand how these experiences affect students and which engagements have the most positive impact. The team tested a battery of educational activities as part of their large national survey, the National Survey of Student Engagement (NSSE). The NSSE is administered at hundreds of colleges each year, gathering data on student performance in higher education, how students spend their time in and out of the classroom, and the ways students develop learning outcomes such as critical thinking. After analyzing the results, the team released what has become known as the list of high-impact practices or HIPs (Kuh, 2008).

Of the list of HIPs, researchers identified a subset that take students beyond the classroom and have particularly impactful results for student success. These core applied and experiential high-impact activities include internships, undergraduate research, service-learning courses, and study abroad. Each of these will be addressed below, along with other educational activities that include the characteristics of HIPs.

What is important about high-impact practices is that they are associated with "a range of positive outcomes for students, especially for students historically underrepresented in higher education" (Kuh et al., 2017, p. 9). When students engage in at least one of these activities, they tend to have stronger academic performance, increased graduation rates, and report higher degrees of satisfaction and learning, including their ability to problem solve (Kuh et al., 2017). High-quality experiential learning can increase students' motivation, curiosity, confidence, self-directed learning, and engagement in and out of class during their time in higher education. Experiential learning can empower students to see how their courses and college activities can help them make an impact in the world.

High-impact practices are also important for student success because they deepen engagement with campus; they require hands-on and often collaborative learning experiences. They shrink the "psychological size of the campus" because students are in close proximity with faculty, staff, and their peers while they work on a substantial task over an extended period of time (Kuh et al., 2017, p. 12). HIPs build connections and community for students—it would be difficult for a student to be anonymous while engaging in a high-impact practice (Kuh et al., 2017). In short, high-impact practices help students feel that they belong and matter.

Experiential learning has the potential to help students find their passions and clarify goals, build their professional skills and networks, and deepen their experiences. When students participate in multiple experiential learning opportunities, the gains are magnified (Finley & McNair, 2013). Of course, the impacts on student success depend on the quality of the HIP; a poorly designed and brief internship with little challenge does not produce the same impacts as a deeply engaging and challenging internship with frequent student reflection.

Research even suggests that participation in experiential learning can elevate students' postgraduation outcomes, potentially increasing the likelihood of a student securing a place in graduate school or in the workforce after graduation (Miller et al., 2017). Researchers have found that students who participate in undergraduate research, for instance, are more likely to apply and be accepted to graduate school than their peers who did not participate in undergraduate research, just as a student who completes a paid internship is more likely to secure employment after graduation than a student who does not have such an experience.

Consider Sam, a student who went to class consistently, took diligent notes, but never tried to talk to his professors outside of class and rarely spoke up during class itself. He spent a fair amount of time studying, so his grades were good. When he wasn't in class, he was happy to play video games and hang out with friends. He did not join any student organizations, nor did he get involved in other ways. Sam wanted to work at a large company after he graduated. As he went through the application process, though, he realized that he was getting few interviews. One interviewer gave him feedback: While Sam's grades were okay, other candidates had a wider breadth of experiences and were able to articulate the skills they'd developed through them. These students had published research papers, held internships on their campuses, and could demonstrate strong transferable skills that the companies desired. Sam, by contrast, hadn't built up these skills by virtue of simply attending class. Even within his classes, he'd struggled to connect his learning to the real world, unlike his peers who were already gaining practical experience. As a result, Sam was being outcompeted.

As we saw above, high-impact practices can be very powerful learning experiences. However, participation in them among college students is not evenly distributed. Despite improvements in the United States and elsewhere, disparities in participation in career-building experiential learning, like internships, undergraduate research, and study abroad persist (Finley & McNair, 2013). Underserved students, including transfer students from community colleges, lower-income students, African American and Latinx students, and those who are the first generation in their families to attend college, participate in experiential learning at lower rates than their non-underrepresented peers (Finley & McNair, 2013). Students with greater financial and other resources often have the capacity to build their skills, professional networks, and resumes through participating in several experiential learning opportunities before they graduate. These could be an unpaid congressional internship in Washington, D.C.; study abroad in Europe; and a research project in New York. However, students, particularly underserved students, may face awareness, mentorship, financial, and other obstacles that can hinder participation.

That said, there are colleges that have robust infrastructure, programming, and support to engage all their students in experiential learning. Some colleges, such as Elon University, have comprehensive, required engagement across the various types of experiential learning, while other colleges may have a special emphasis on one or two types. Below we explore each form of experiential learning in more depth.

WORK-BASED LEARNING: INTERNSHIPS AND CO-OPS

Internships engage students in learning experiences with an organization in a professional setting, providing students valuable work experiences that enrich their curricular and co-curricular college experiences. Often, internships are related to a student's major or career goals. As such, they can help provide students professional clarity while building key skills that enable them to launch successfully from college.

High-quality internships increase the likelihood of securing employment right after college, particularly as companies commonly use internships as ways to find potential employees (Miller et al., 2017). In fact, a 2018 national survey by the National Association of Colleges and Employers (NACE) found that employers hired slightly more than half of their interns as full-time employees (2018). Another national survey of employers found that nearly all of those surveyed would be "more likely to hire a recent graduate who has held an internship or apprenticeship with a company or organization" (Pasquerella, 2019).

Internships, like all other forms of experiential learning, can vary in length and quality, with longer, immersive, and challenging roles typically being more formative than others. One example of this kind of longer, work-based learning is the co-op. These usually last at least a semester, and provide full-time, paid work experience directly related to a student's major and career interests.

Many majors at a college may offer academic credit for internships or co-ops, and some may even require them for graduation. For instance, a college may require business majors to do an internship to graduate; a nursing major is typically required to undertake a clinical practicum in which they work and train in a healthcare setting, such as a hospital, for a semester or more. Other colleges or majors, however, may not offer any kind of academic credit for students who complete an internship or co-op, sometimes making it more difficult for students to integrate an internship into their academic pathway. This may suggest that the college or major prioritizes other forms of learning.

Colleges may also offer job-shadowing opportunities. These are typically 1-day to 1-week experiences in which students observe or engage in a project at an organization. Often these programs are organized by a college, and the shadow experience is with alumni or organizations who are looking at the program as an employee recruitment mechanism. Other short-term opportunities include micro-internships, which are project-based opportunities with employers generally lasting 10–40 hours total.

Sometimes work-based learning opportunities aren't with an existing company—instead, colleges provide resources for students to create their own start-up company or organization. Unlike a traditional internship with an employer, students may have the ability to be entrepreneurs and draw on the resources of a college, financial and otherwise. A member of a college's faculty or a community member will typically mentor the student and provide expertise.

Several dimensions affect the access to and quality of these work-based learning opportunities. The most common reasons students report being unsatisfied with an internship are a lack of meaningful responsibilities (i.e., just getting coffee and running errands) and a lack of professional development (NACE, 2017). When a student considers internship opportunities coordinated by the college, it is helpful to ask how the college chooses and approves these programs. Has the college ensured that participating students will have meaningful work to build their skills? Will there be appropriate supervision and mentorship? Or will the students be treated like inexpensive help? You can also assess what guidance and mentorship is provided throughout this process from the college: helping find and secure an internship, setting goals, and debriefing after the experience to reflect on learning and integrate into college and beyond. In addition, it is important to assess what funding, if any, the college provides to support students.

Another aspect to consider is whether the work-based learning experience is paid. Research has found that students with paid internship and co-op experiences are more likely to be offered full-time employment and receive higher salary offers than their peers who complete unpaid experiences (NACE, 2016). However, a significant minority of internships are unpaid. In 2018, for example, 40% of internships were unpaid (NACE, 2018).

Prospective students should examine the support colleges have in place for all these work-based learning opportunities. Students should assess the likelihood of engaging in one or more forms of work-based learning opportunities at any given college. Some colleges prompt students to complete an internship only in their last few semesters in college, but even more junior students can benefit from the perspectives, skills, and professional directional that work-based learning can provide.

Let's consider the cases of Eileen and Phillip. Going into college, Eileen was a communications major. She wanted to work for a news network after college and thought she would be a producer. She decided to intern over the summer with a local news station. She discovered that producing wasn't for her; the work environment felt too rushed for her to feel comfortable. Even though she was disappointed to not like the day-to-day realities of television producing, she was grateful for the experience: Eileen knew that her major no longer aligned with her career aspirations. She was able to shift gears and change her major easily, without negative implications on her academic progress.

Phillip, on the other hand, waited until the summer before his senior year to intern. His internship was at a juvenile justice center. Like Eileen, Phillip realized that his intended career field wasn't one he wanted to work in. He discovered that working in the center was emotionally exhausting in ways he hadn't anticipated and that the profession wouldn't be sustainable for him. But unlike Eileen, he felt he was too far into his studies to change tracks. Phillip felt backed into a corner and regretted not finding professional experience earlier.

UNDERGRADUATE RESEARCH AND CREATIVE ACTIVITY

In addition to teaching classes, professors often conduct research and engage in creative endeavors. They try to understand and solve important problems to our society. Research happens in every major and discipline. In biology it could include a lab studying cancer cells; in social sciences it could mean seeking to understand voter turnout patterns; in the arts and humanities, it could take the form of composing and performing an original piece of music or translating ancient texts and understanding their cultural contexts.

Research isn't just for professors or people getting a doctoral degree—undergraduate students can and often should engage in research, too. Students can learn a great deal by doing research and by helping to create new knowledge. The Council on Undergraduate Research, the U.S. national organization promoting undergraduate research, defines undergraduate research as "an inquiry or investigation conducted by an undergraduate student that makes an original intellectual or creative contribution to the discipline" (CUR, n.d.). Often, undergraduate research takes the form of a student serving as an assistant to a faculty member or graduate student, helping them conduct their research projects. At a higher level, it can include a student conducting their own research that is mentored and guided by a faculty member or graduate student. An excellent college empowers students to conduct independent research and gives them the resources to do so, as will be explored later in this chapter.

Students can earn academic credit or pay for conducting undergraduate research, or simply serve on a volunteer basis. Students can serve on undergraduate research projects for a semester or even multiple years during their bachelor's degree. They can also present their research at on-campus research conferences and travel to special undergraduate research conferences. Some even present their research at professional conferences alongside professors and graduate students. The most advanced undergraduate researchers will co-author research publications with faculty members or even publish their own research in national and international research publications.

Engagement in undergraduate research has clear benefits, especially when the student is in their first or second year of college (Mayhew et al., 2016). It can help students clarify their major and improve academic performance in the classroom. It can also help students build mentorship relationships with faculty members for professional guidance and letters of recommendation. More broadly, these experiences can elevate a student's self-efficacy and sense of belonging on campus and cultivate their capacities to think independently.

Additionally, many graduate school programs expect their applicants to have engaged in undergraduate research because the graduate programs themselves are research-intensive. As a result, students who engage in research as undergraduates may be stronger, more competitive applicants to graduate school programs. Undergraduate research can also be helpful to students entering the job force. Students can communicate their research experiences to employers to help demonstrate their capacity to understand and analyze complex problems and present solutions.

Diana is one such student who engaged in undergraduate research. She participated in a research program her first year of college, as the sole research assistant for a professor in the sociology department. Prior to attending college, she had never envisioned herself doing research. She associated it with science fair and chemistry labs and had never imagined research projects that aligned with her own interests. Dianna had also come from a small town and felt lost at a large college. Conducting undergraduate research proved to be transformational for her. The research skills she gained while carrying out and analyzing interviews with low-income families meant that undertaking academic projects was less daunting. Working closely with a professor not only provided her with direct mentorship, but also helped her build the confidence to build relationships with other professors. Because undergraduate research cultivated academic and personal growth, Diana felt more connected to her college as she progressed through the year.

Access to undergraduate research differs across colleges. Larger colleges that conduct lots of research (also known as R1 universities, as discussed in Chapter 2) tend to have more varied opportunities for students to engage in research at the college than smaller, primarily undergraduate institutions. There are billions of dollars in research activities at colleges each year funded by federal and state grants and the institutions themselves.

How does a student engage in undergraduate research? The old model, which is still seen in higher education, is that a student finds a faculty member on their own, visits them in person or contacts them, and asks if they have any research opportunities for undergraduates available. Sometimes this works, but sadly, students often get turned down because the professor does not have the time or available space or other resources to mentor a student researcher. This may be especially common in the health science areas in which so many students seek undergraduate research opportunities to enhance applications for graduate school and medical school. As we saw in Chapter 4 around faculty office hours, it can be similarly intimidating and unfamiliar for students to ask if they can help with a faculty member's research, which prevents many students from doing so in the first place. In some cases, a faculty member may propose that a high-performing student in their class consider joining them in their research.

The best colleges for undergraduate research facilitate opportunities for engagement in undergraduate research through structured programs. One of the earliest and best-known such program is the Undergraduate Research Opportunity Program at the University of Michigan. The program supports scores of first and second-year students, as well as transfer students, in peer-mentored programming that helps pair students with faculty research projects for a year (University of Michigan, n.d.). Students present their research to the college community at an end-of-year conference. The program has been replicated at several other colleges across the United States and beyond.

Undergraduate research does not happen only in distinct programs; it can also manifest in the curriculum and in specific courses. Some colleges intentionally design their curriculum to build students' research skills, often starting with courses that expose student to basic concepts in research and build their research skills, such as through helping students draft a research-informed final course paper. A curriculum or major may culminate in the final year with asking students to conduct their own original research or creative endeavor, such as in the capstone courses discussed in Chapter 3. One long-standing example of such a curricular focus on research is at Princeton University. Princeton's curriculum seeks to challenge students "to develop their scholarly interests and to evolve as independent thinkers," culminating that process with a Senior Thesis Program in which all students produce an original research project (Princeton University, n.d.).

SERVICE LEARNING

In service-learning courses, students volunteer in partnership with a community-based organization, such as a non-profit, as an integrated part of the course. The community, in a sense, becomes part of the classroom, giving students direct experience with the issues they are studying and providing organizations with student and faculty time and expertise. The courses challenge students to analyze problems in the community, empowering them with a deeper and more complex understanding of the challenges facing communities. Students are guided in their reflection through the process. Service-learning courses can also improve a student's postgraduation outcomes. Just as national surveys of employers have found for internships, employers at nonprofits say they "are much more likely to hire recent graduates

who have community-based or service-learning experience" (Pasquerella, 2019).

At the University of Nebraska–Omaha, for example, their Service Learning Academy coordinates many service-learning courses
throughout the college (UNO, 2019). Students in a business ethics
course partner with community agencies for the entirety of the semester and conduct ethics audits for their partner organizations to
help them implement best practices around ethical decisionmaking
processes. In a course around early childhood development, meanwhile, students work with children in underserved communities to
build literacy skills and a love of reading. Students develop and lead
lessons for the children, empowering the students and the children's
caregiver to integrate similar skill-building in their daily lives.

Research suggests these kinds of courses, done well, enrich student learning and also imbue them with a sense of civic engagement
and service to others that carries with them to and through college
and beyond as citizens and employees.

STUDY ABROAD

International education, in which a student goes out of the country
to pursue an educational endeavor, has been a longstanding part of
the higher education landscape. There can be deep, powerful impacts
from international education, particularly study abroad experiences
that immerse and challenge students in new environments. International study is also important as a vehicle to develop students as global citizens and potential employees, able to live and work in diverse
communities.

As with all educational experiences, quality matters, and some kinds
of study abroad are more formative than others. Immersive, long-term
experiences in which students are challenged in unfamiliar environments and build relationships with diverse others foster significant impacts on the student (O'Shea, 2014). The length of overseas programs
correlates positively with the permanence of their effects in developing
students' sense of self; effects can last a lifetime (Dwyer, 2004).

To enrich the learning experience, colleges should offer support
before, during, and after the study abroad experiences. Importantly,
students should receive guidance to reflect on their learning during
their experience, and the college should help students articulate their
learning and skills development.

There are several types of study abroad, usually organized by the college itself or through an outside organization that helps facilitate the experiences for students.

- **Traditional Study Abroad:** Students travel to another country and take courses, often with the support of on-site faculty and staff. Faculty and staff support the students and plan educational experiences in the local community or region. These experiences range from short- to long-term. Students may study in Florence for a week over spring break, for example, or may study there for an entire summer term.
- **Exchanges:** Students enroll at an overseas college for a semester or year, transferring the credit back to their home institution upon completion of the academic term. Often, colleges have agreements in which students pay the same tuition rate while overseas as they would at their home institution.
- **International Internships:** Students work as interns with companies, non-profits, or governments while abroad. A college may have staff in London who facilitate internship placements in the British Parliament, the British Museum, or Barclays Bank.
- **International Research Experiences:** Students work as a research assistant overseas with a faculty member or conduct their own research. A student might travel to Brazil to conduct ecological research on the Amazon rainforest for their senior thesis.
- **International Service Learning:** Students volunteer in an overseas community setting in partnership with an organization connected to learning outcomes and often course topics.
- **First Semester Abroad/First Year Abroad:** Students spend their first semester or first year of college overseas studying at a study abroad site and earning credit.
- **Educational Gap Years:** Students typically defer their first year in college to engage in experiential learning for a semester or year. While gap years are not exclusively done overseas, it is common for students to travel internationally and volunteer while abroad.

There are several benefits that have emerged from participation in study abroad. One of these is skill development. Through study abroad, students can become better communicators and problem solvers. Students may also become more creative and adaptable, as they learn to adjust to new situations and cultures (Maddux & Galinsky, 2009). Study abroad can also prompt students to reflect and develop their own sense of identity, and to make friends and develop their professional network on a global scale.

Additionally, study abroad can have a positive impact on students after the conclusion of their experience, and even after they graduate. Numerous surveys of alumni and employers say that the study abroad experience often made a difference in hiring decisions, expanded the kinds of jobs alumni considered, and cultivated the skills that helped alumni excel in their jobs, leading to professional advancement (Institute of International Education, 2017).

By examining two students' experiences, we can better understand the benefits and potential pitfalls of study abroad experiences. Mia took a summer semester in Barcelona, Spain. She and her roommates—all Americans from the same college—spent time exclusively with other students from their school. Mia wanted to improve her language fluency. But because she was talking only to her roommates, she only spoke English while she was abroad. The program itself failed to build in opportunities for cross-cultural engagement or learning. Looking back, she was disappointed in how little the program pushed her to grow.

Meanwhile, Caleb studied abroad in Valencia, Spain. At the orientation meeting, the professors emphasized the importance of stepping outside of one's comfort zone and maximizing the experience of being abroad. In the months before he left for Spain, Caleb took a pre-departure training program. Once a week, he and the other study abroad participants would meet. A professor from his college's study abroad office facilitated discussion about the culture, history, and modern landscape in Valencia. They also gave him resources to continue learning on his own, like a pocket guide with basic Spanish language. Moreover, his college helped him find an internship placement in Valencia, where he was immersed in a different culture and spoke Spanish every day. Although he spent time with his roommates, he also spent time on his own exploring the city. Built into the program itself were trips to less touristy parts of the city, where he was able to develop a deeper understanding of the area and cultural practices of people who lived there.

ASSESSING A COLLEGE'S APPLIED AND EXPERIENTIAL LEARNING

As you consider different colleges and experiential learning opportunities, you'll want to be thinking about ways in which colleges make experiential learning accessible and impactful. It is fundamental that a college provide the mentorship, guidance, and connections to help students find high-quality opportunities. A thoughtful advisor can help a student map out possible experiences through their time in college, reflecting and changing as needed along the way: a research experience in the first year of college, a service-learning course during the second year, study abroad in the second summer, and an internship in the third year. Since there are many curricular requirements for each major, an advisor can help a student plan experiential learning opportunities without compromising progress toward their degree.

Another thing to look for is the likelihood of participating in experiential learning at a given college. Many majors or colleges have experiential learning required as part of their degree pathway. Colleges may publicly showcase their experiential learning opportunities and their students' participation rates on their websites and promotional materials. Outside organizations also surface data on experiential learning at individual colleges. The Institute of International Education, for example, publishes an annual Open Doors report which aggregates data on colleges' study abroad participation and the diversity of opportunities provided to students. (Some of IIE's data analysis can be accessed freely via https://www.iie.org/opendoors.) You can also ask colleges directly about experiential learning, student participation, and any gaps in engagement. You should look for the breadth of experiential learning opportunities and programs provided by the college, and the funding they offer to help students participate in them. These questions will help you see if opportunities are unevenly distributed to certain majors or student populations.

Something else to consider is where a college is located relative to opportunities for experiential learning. Location is not the end-all-be-all to experiential learning, but it does impact how accessible it may be. A college located in a major city may have a wide range of internships, research positions, or avenues for service readily available. A student who attends college in Washington, D.C., may have robust opportunities to intern at non-profits, think tanks, and government offices. However, colleges geared toward student success, regardless of location, will have mechanisms to help students find and secure experiential learning positions. Any college has the capacity to enable experiential learning in their local communities, across the country, or internationally. Undergraduate research can occur on any campus, and there will always be opportunities to intern somewhere, particularly when a college provides sufficient guidance, connections, and funding support. For students who wish to engage in opportunities outside of their college's location, the summer is the most common time to travel. With assistance from their college, many students intern in different cities and conduct research at other colleges.

WHAT STUDENTS CAN DO BEFORE COLLEGE TO PREPARE

Given the importance of experiential learning, students may want to prepare for opportunities before they even start college. Where possible, students can engage in experiential learning in high school, undertaking internships; service-learning and volunteering; studying or traveling overseas; and even doing research—sometimes in partnership with a teacher or a faculty member at a college. These experiences can be highly formative and make a student more ready and competitive when applying for opportunities in college. Students can build on their experiential learning opportunities from high school once they reach college. A student who starts a research project in their senior year of high school may want to continue and deepen their inquiry once they begin college, for instance.

Students may also engage in an educational gap year before starting college, in which they defer enrollment for a year after graduating high school, as mentioned earlier. During such a gap year, students can engage in internships, service learning, research, and other forms of experiential learning, thus building a set of formative experiences and challenging themselves before they start college. Educational gap years go beyond the simple act of waiting to enroll in college for a year; they are purposeful and deliberate, designed to foster educational growth and personal and professional development. Taking a year off without bolstering it with meaningful activity can make it less likely that a student will ultimately enroll in college, unlike the educational gap year, which boosts outcomes. The Gap Year Association offers some quality assurance for gap year programs, as programs they accredit must meet the association's standards (GYA, n.d.). Students who take an educational gap year tend to do well in college, with high academic performance, motivation, and engagement (O'Shea, 2014).

> ### THREE GUIDING QUESTIONS TO ASK ABOUT
> ### APPLIED AND EXPERIENTIAL LEARNING
>
> 1. To what extent are various forms of experiential learning accessible and common among students at the college?
> 2. To what extent does the college provide mentorship, guidance, structured programming, and support for engaging in experiential learning?
> 3. To what extent is the experiential learning facilitated by the college of high quality and high impact?

Table 5.1. A Rubric for Evaluating a College's Applied and Experiential Learning

Level	Indicators
Excellent	College has a broad range of high-quality applied and experiential learning opportunities across students' college careers, with integrated mentorship and reflection; high participation rates or required participation exists, potentially integrated into students' curricular pathways; sufficient financial and advising support enables all students to participate, even in multiple programs.
Good	College has widespread and varied opportunities for applied and experiential learning; opportunities are offered for students across all years and potentially for academic credit; advising, guidance, and financial support are provided by the college, but not enough to meet the full needs of students; participation rates are strong, but varied.
Average	College has several different programs and opportunities for applied and experiential learning; programs reach segments of the population, but gaps exist; quality of the programming and guidance is varied; financial aid and academic credit opportunities are present for some but insufficient.
Fair	College has some programs of varying quality for applied and experiential learning with limited participation; gaps exist among the student body, mostly among underserved students; there is limited financial support and guidance to support student participation.
Poor	College has few applied and experiential learning opportunities; students are largely left on their own to find experiences, with low participation rates; little financial and advising support or mentorship exists; alignment with curriculum or possibilities for academic credit for experiences is minimal.

CHAPTER 6

Does It Matter Who Your Friends Are?

Engagement and Leadership Development

When Katia first came to college, she didn't know anybody. Because she chose a college outside her home state, most of her friends and family were hours and hours away. She was worried about finding a group of people to hang out with, and relieved that her roommate in her residence hall seemed friendly. Katia and her roommate spent most of their time with other people on the same floor of her residence hall, and that soon became Katia's main friend group. In the months that followed, though, Katia got the feeling that this friend group wasn't really right for her. Katia enjoyed her classes, but whenever she tried to talk about them, her roommate would laugh, say chemistry was boring, and change the subject. None of the gang was in any clubs, and Katia realized that she wasn't involved with anything on campus either. The people she admired on campus were active in student government or in intramural sports. As her first year ended, Katia realized that her friend group was mostly a friend group of convenience. They weren't bad people, but they weren't pushing her to grow or even interested in the same things Katia was. As she entered her sophomore year, Katia resolved to stay friendly with her old roommate, but seek out new connections on campus.

A common saying is that a student's time in college is the best years of their life and that they should enjoy it to the fullest. Students are meeting new people, joining clubs, building relationships, engaging in social and recreational activities, sharing common experiences, and more. For many students, these activities can prompt reflection on their values, priorities, and clarify who they want to be in life.

To some people, extracurricular or recreational activities may seem peripheral to the core part of a student's college experience. But these can be powerful components of a student's learning. Students inspire and influence each other to behave in certain ways, help form habits and certain values, question each other's held assumptions, shape identities, and develop new reasoning and ways of thinking as they make their way in the world (Mayhew et al., 2016). It's no surprise, then, that many students report that much of their learning and development in college was a result of their interactions with peers and out-of-class activities and programming.

But how does this happen?

Colleges can intentionally facilitate these kinds of engagements and relationships, or they can sit back and hope they happen organically. But often these sorts of engagements and relationships are sparked with facilitation. Since a sense of belonging is so important to student success, we should pay close attention to social networks in college, how they develop and function, and the various approaches colleges use to build these networks.

Research shows how important it is for students to have a diverse social network. This means it has diversity of thought, background, socioeconomic status, and more. All of these diverse perspectives can challenge students' ways of understanding themselves and the world around them and propel their educational growth. Students who interact only with a homogenous group (i.e., people who think, talk, and look like them) develop at slower rates across various personal, moral, and intellectual dimensions than those who have more diverse, heterogeneous social networks. In other words, when we build relationships with new people, particularly those who are not like us, we develop more. And when we have these abilities, we are better able to excel in the diverse and ever-changing landscapes of our work and civic lives.

When researchers track the moral reasoning of students who developed close friends while in college, compared to those who report almost exclusively maintaining their close friendships from high school, they see more advanced levels of moral reasoning for those who develop new college friendships (Derryberry & Thoma, 2000). The gap in the development of moral reasoning, as seen through the differing ways students consider and justify moral decisions, increases over time between these two groups, as students with more diverse social networks are challenged with new perspectives and assumptions. Likewise, research shows a similar pattern for students in understanding of and appreciation for diverse worldviews—making friends with people of various religious and personal backgrounds deepens one's appreciation for the diversity of the world (Interfaith Youth Core, 2019).

To be sure, close, supportive friendships are important for the development of students. But how a students' social network is composed is important. If a student has a network made up of different sorts of people who may not be friends with each other (e.g., friends from various classes, a sports club, and a study abroad trip), they develop more than those with very dense social networks—in other words, those with tight friendship groups composed of those who all know each other, such as in a high school clique.

The challenge in developing this kind of diverse peer network is that students tend to stay within their social comfort zones, to self-segregate into groups of sameness and engage with those who think, talk, and look like themselves. Why? Because it can be uncomfortable to engage with people who challenge our perspectives or backgrounds.

But as the research shows, engaging and building meaningful relationships with those who are different from ourselves is vitally important. Doing this forces us to inhabit the paradigm of another, to see the world as they do, and to reevaluate our assumptions about ourselves and the world around us (O'Shea, 2014). Building this kind of empathy, what scholar Martha Nussbaum called narrative imagination, is a central tenet of being a citizen and employee in the world today (Nussbaum, 1998). When we can and regularly do imagine the world from another's perspective, it allows us to see how the decisions we make impact other communities and groups, not just our own.

Immersing oneself in a college learning environment that fosters narrative imagination depends, in part, on the composition of the student body, and how students engage with each other. One way colleges facilitate diverse student interaction is by enrolling students from various backgrounds in the first place. Given the educational growth that comes from engaging with new and diverse relationships, prospective students should look for colleges with a student body that has sufficient diversity to cultivate these relationships. With a diverse student body, students may be more likely to be in courses, live in residence halls, or participate in student clubs and organizations with students who will collectively push each other to develop and grow.

But just looking at the demographic statistics of a student body may not be enough. To fully realize the benefits of diversity, students have to build actual, deep, and meaningful relationships with diverse others. Colleges that are intentional about harnessing the power of diversity as an educational force have a number of ways of doing so and infuse that work throughout the institution: how they structure residential life, how they build community and set up student programming, and how they facilitate conversations about diverse issues.

Despite the promise of the benefits of engagement of various kinds, college shouldn't feel like a series of utilitarian calculations of how every relationship or experience could contribute to your educational growth. College can and should be fun, and it can also be a time to enjoy seemingly purposeless relationships. But being mindful and thoughtful of the broader trends in your engagement, and being introspective and critical of how you are growing and being influenced by others and your environment, can be a guiding practice as you grow through higher education. After all, so much of college is students forming themselves in connection to everyone around them.

CULTURE AND FIT

Some people believe there is one right college for them: a perfect fit waiting to be discovered or a dream school that will punch their ticket to success. But it's clear that there are many "right" colleges for students, and students of all sorts can be successful at a host of different colleges. Colleges do not have singular cultures. They are diverse, full of niche communities and ways of engaging in student life. The culture of the robotics club might be very different from that of the theater club, for instance. Students can, particularly with the right kind of facilitated activities and programming at the college, find their sense of place within many institutions. In short, fit happens. Students' sense of belonging and satisfaction with the campus tends to grow over time, as students find and engage with peer groups, interest groups, courses, mentors, communities, and programs that help make fit happen.

Colleges, like all communities and institutions, have cultural practices and norms that shape the behavior and expectations of their members. Certain colleges have points of emphasis in whom they attract and in how they encourage students to act and spend their time. American football may dominate much of a culture at a campus during the fall and basketball in the spring, while another college might pay very little attention to sporting events. Similarly, a college may offer robust speaker series, be more heavily involved in politics or activism, or have widespread fine arts programming, with on-campus museums and operas, plays, or musical productions.

It is hard to really assess the culture of a place, particularly without immersion within it. A college may share data from surveys of their students about campus life they've conducted or by national organizations on their institutional research website, or by request. You can look at websites for a college, their student newspaper, at events and guest speakers on campus, and other student-level activities to get a window into what daily life at the college may be like. And if you do visit a college, mixing with the current students, eating with them in the dining hall, sitting in on a class (if possible), asking students about how they spend time, and observing the kind of conversations students are having can all be ways to get a sense of what is happening in student life.

Prospective students often wonder how the size of a college affects its culture. Colleges, especially larger ones, are generally diverse enough that they don't have monolithic cultures or singular activities. Even if you go to a school that seems focused around sporting events, there will still be communities within the college that engage in other activities. The size of a college does not necessarily indicate the intimacy of the learning environment and the campus experience. A very small college produces inevitable closeness, but larger colleges have smaller, more intimate communities. While it may be easier to access them at smaller colleges, larger colleges do have smaller, more intimate communities within them, as students build smaller circles in their residence halls, in clubs, and in courses. The surrounding community of a college can also influence the culture of colleges; colleges do not operate in a vacuum and students engage with the community and people around them. Understanding the culture, politics, and other dynamics of the surrounding community can be important in understanding the context in which a student will study.

SENSE OF BELONGING AND IMPOSTER SYNDROME

Many students in college will ask themselves this question at some point: Do I feel like I belong here? Feeling like you belong and that you matter is fundamental to human well-being and student success (Baumeister & Leary, 1995). Researchers and higher education professionals refer to this feeling as a sense of belonging. Specifically, Strayhorn (2018) defines sense of belonging as "students' perceived social support on campus, a feeling or sensation of connectedness, the experience of mattering or feeling cared about, accepted, respected, valued by, and important to the group (e.g., campus community) or others on campus (e.g., faculty, peers)" (p. 3). A sense of belonging is critical to helping students engage with the college and stay there until they graduate. While questioning whether you belong is common across all student populations, racial-ethnic minorities and first-generation students are often more likely to report a lower sense of belonging in higher education, particularly if they attend a college where they're underrepresented.

If students report that they don't feel that they belong at the college, then they are at a higher risk of leaving college. It makes it harder for them to thrive—to persist, to take risks, to share their thoughts and engage, to explore and experiment. Conversely, if students feel like they belong at the college, they have higher rates of personal and academic success, with improved graduation rates, engagement, and mental health (Gopalan & Brady, 2019). College communities that are not particularly welcoming and inclusive to the full diversity of their student body can exacerbate feelings of disconnection.

Related to a sense of belonging is the concept of *imposter syndrome*. Imposter syndrome occurs when someone feels like they don't deserve to be in a situation—in this case, at the college. In other words, they feel that they are an imposter and someone is going to find out that they are not supposed to be there or in their role. Did they make a mistake in admitting me? Am I really supposed to be here?

Imposter syndrome can be especially prominent among students who are the first generation in their families to go to college, whose sense of belonging in college may be lower to begin with. But imposter syndrome isn't limited to college students; professors and many other professionals report feeling this as they start their careers. A bad case of imposter syndrome can damage a student's performance and engagement in college and contribute to a low sense of belonging. In addition, it may hinder students' willingness to apply for awards, scholarships, programs, and competitive fellowships. It is common to hear students express that they could never win major fellowships like the Rhodes Scholarship because they look at the winners and say they could never "be them" or "do what they did." Thus, students select themselves out of the process when in fact many could have been highly competitive candidates.

Cultivating the conditions that allow students to feel that their college has their back and that they are part of the institution is paramount. Colleges can help address both psychological patterns of sense of belonging and imposter syndrome through an inclusive and welcoming culture. Faculty, staff, and peers can help students see that they have the traits to be successful at the college and that they belong there. A diverse faculty and student body can help students from historically underrepresented and minority backgrounds see themselves at the college. And professors can also normalize and de-stigmatize anxieties around belonging by sharing their own stories and feelings. Many colleges have programs to celebrate first-generation students and faculty, such as First to College campaigns. Colleges can also encourage students to seek guidance early if they begin to have these patterns of thinking.

Some colleges are better than others at fostering a sense of belonging. These colleges build intentional supports and programming, often more intensive in the first year or two of college, to help students build the new skills of successfully navigating the college environment. College staff and leadership can also actively work to advance antiracism, equity, and inclusion efforts within the college. Working at the institutional level, college personnel can work toward ensuring that the college's policies, practices, and culture are addressing systemic racism and injustices. An important dimension of this is ensuring students can fully participate in all the ways we have explored in this book thus far to engage students in experiential learning, in proactive advising and community-building programming, in courses that integrate active learning, and more. These can all help build students' connection to the college and feelings of empowerment.

Throughout the rest of this chapter, we will examine different avenues of student engagement that can contribute to student success, including learning communities, student government, and more. All of these offer students ways of meeting each other, forming friendships, and building a sense of belonging.

LEARNING COMMUNITIES: MAKING COLLEGE FEEL SMALLER

Colleges can help students build community from the very beginning through various forms of *learning communities*. Learning communities vary, but they often bring together small groups of students with common interests, majors, or activities and engage them in some structured programming, typically during the first year of college. For instance, a first-year experience program may have students meet weekly in sessions facilitated by staff and a peer mentor. Students in this program are introduced to the college and its various resources and perform activities together. In addition, and what is often the most powerful part, students often take a few courses together, giving students a built-in social and peer network. In effect, they will know 15 or 20 other students within several courses, even if those other courses are very large. Because learning communities help students build community in the context of their courses, they help students integrate their academic and social lives, and they can have powerful effects on student performance (Smith, 2004).

One prominent example of how a college builds learning communities is the University of Texas at Austin's 360 Connections program, which engages nearly every new student in a small, peer-mentored learning community of some kind (University of Texas at Austin, n.d.). The program provides an inventory of 360 Connection opportunities for students, tailoring some to specific majors or interests. Students work with their advisor to determine which of the learning communities is a good fit for their interests and needs. The students who may need more support are aligned with the most intensive communities, perhaps a residential hall–based learning community where students are living together, taking a few courses together, and engaging in other out-of-class programming together.

HONORS PROGRAMS

Honors programs are a well-established form of academic sub-community within colleges. These can be institution-wide honors programs, or honors programs within a specific major, and are generally targeted at students who are particularly high-achieving or had strong academic performance in high school. These programs can provide special courses and curriculum, often taught by honors faculty members. There may also be honors-specific programming and community-building activities, study abroad experiences, undergraduate research and creative activities, and other opportunities. Honors programs may offer students priority course registration so that they can register for courses before other students and ensure they get the classes they want or need. These programs connect students with their similarly high-achieving and ambitious peers to provide stimulating conversation across majors and provide a powerful educational community.

Honors programs serve many purposes. For the college, honors programs can help recruit high-achieving students who might not otherwise have considered attending the institution, particularly if there is a special scholarship for being in an honors program. Being accepted to honors programs can bring a certain prestige and exclusivity for students. And since these programs can provide an intimate and perhaps more intellectually challenging experience for students, students may choose an honors program at a less-prestigious institution over attending a more-prestigious institution without acceptance to its honors program.

Additionally, these programs can help advance the full educational growth of high-achieving students. High-achieving students may need additional challenges and stimulation beyond what a traditional college experience may provide. It's possible for a student to attend a college and get good grades and not be challenged to grow to their full potential. Rigorous honors programs can help colleges retain students by deeply engaging them with their educational experience.

Participation in these merit-based academic programs can also foster a sense of belonging in its students, facilitating a rich social and intellectual community that pulls together students from across campus. Honors programs often host events planned to build this sense of community, from movie screenings to intramural sports matches. When these programs have a physical space or building, like Florida State University's Honors, Scholars, and Fellows House, it can make building those bonds even easier.

That said, the kind of educational experiences that honors programs can provide are beneficial for all students, within and outside of honors programs. In this way, honors programs model the kind of education that colleges should strive to provide for their entire student population.

RESIDENTIAL LIFE

Many colleges offer students the opportunity to live on campus. In fact, at some colleges it is required for the first year or longer. Colleges have largely moved away from calling these residencies "dorms," as they once did. Instead, colleges will say that a student is in "residential life" and living in a "residence hall." By using this language, colleges are trying to signal that these environments can provide educational and social value.

So, should students live on campus? The residence hall options might be small, older buildings that need remodeling. Why not live off-campus in a nice, new, and spacious apartment? Research tells us that students should aim to live on campus, at least for their first year.

Living in a college residence hall often lifts students' retention and graduation rates; when students live on campus, they are spending more time in formative, educational settings (Mayhew et al., 2016). They are also closer to campus and educational activities, which increases their participation in them. Moreover, the communal nature of residential life facilitates the kind of social network formation, the late-night conversations and meals, and the organic relationships that can be so important to student life and education, as discussed earlier in this chapter.

Not all campus residential living situations produce the same positive effects, however. One interesting finding is how differential residential designs can impact student success. Some colleges have constructed residential buildings that mimic high-end apartment complexes with large private rooms and lots of personal space. However, research has found these kinds of residential designs can actually have negative impacts on student success (Fischer, 2017). Why? Because large private spaces encourage students to spend time alone in their room and not engage with others, which can lead to loneliness, lack of sense of belonging and community, and less development through peer conversation. Colleges with smaller rooms, with more inviting common and communal spaces, tend to foster more growth. Community-centric residential life can help facilitate relationships between diverse sets of students and can also increase students' sense of belonging.

In addition, there are many purposeful efforts that illustrate the educational impact of on-campus living. Colleges may offer student learning support services within residence halls, including dedicated spaces and staff to help students collaborate, study, receive tutoring and advising, and more, which can increase access and use of these important forms of learning. Trained residential assistants (RAs) and professional staff are in residence halls to supervise students and provide mediation and advice. If a student is having trouble with their roommate, for example, their RA can be the first line of support. An RA may also be the first to notice that a student is frequently skipping class or having other troubles and can intervene early. Some colleges use the "residential college" model, in which a faculty member and their family will live in the hall to facilitate additional mentorship, education activities, and growth.

Colleges may additionally offer a residential curriculum of sorts within a residence hall. These efforts provide students living in the halls with structured support, intentional connections, learning opportunities, and community-building programming with specific learning outcomes throughout. The curriculum is typically aligned with topics and challenges students are likely to encounter as they begin college. The University of Kentucky's residential curriculum is one such example (University of Kentucky, 2019). Their residential curriculum engages students holistically with inclusion, academic success, health and wellness, self and relational management, and more. By engaging across these topics, students at the University of Kentucky can start building foundational skills for success in college.

Many colleges also have what are called *living learning communities* or themed housing. These take different forms, but generally they are communities within a residence hall with a specific interest or focus. There are living learning communities for students who are studying music, interested in sustainability, or are women in science, to name a few. In a living learning community, the students often take an informal, discussion-based course together, and may also take other key academic courses together connected to their interest area. A faculty or staff member may serve as the leader of these communities. Living learning communities in which students take linked and common courses have been found to be highly impactful for students' development. In fact, living learning communities have been identified as a high-impact practice by researchers because of their positive impacts on student success, like those found in Chapter 5 (Kuh, 2008). If possible, students should look for this kind of educational opportunity in their housing situation in college.

ROOMMATES

Does it matter who students' roommates are? Yes, roommates (and other close friends) can have significant impacts on students' success and life in college overall. They can influence how a student transitions to college, how they spend their time, and what their grade point average is, and more, as research finds. One study found that a studious roommate can have positive impacts on their roommate's academic performance. The researchers found that students who had a studious roommate studied more and had a higher grade point average than those who did not (Mehta et al., 2018).

Research also shows the impact of roommates and drinking on grades. If a student who didn't drink alcohol prior to attending college is randomly paired with a roommate who drinks alcohol, the student who didn't drink is likely to experience a lower grade point average (GPA) by up to a quarter of a point than their peers without a roommate who drinks (Kremer & Levy, 2008). In this study, the research found that if both roommates drink, then the effect on their GPAs was even more pronounced, particularly for males, with up to two-thirds of a point lower. The reduction in GPA persisted through to a second year in college, presumably because habits around alcohol were formed and continued despite the fact that many students were living with different roommates after their first year.

As other research finds, having a roommate of another race reduces prejudice and also leads to students diversifying their friendships. Even years later, students report less prejudice and more easy interaction with diverse groups of people after having a roommate who was a different race or ethnicity from them (Boisjoly et al., 2006). Given the potential implications, selecting roommate(s) thoughtfully can be important for student success.

STUDENT CLUBS

Virtually every college provides opportunities for students to create a student club or organization. Colleges usually have numerous student clubs; at Florida State University, for instance, there are over 750 student clubs and organizations (Florida State University, n.d.). These clubs allow students to join their peers around common interests, ranging from rock climbing; to political activism; to mental health and advocacy; to salsa dancing; to theater, comedy, and music groups; to sports; and much more. Students may also form student associations to build community among students with similar backgrounds, such as the Black Student Union, Asian Student Association, LGBTQ+ student group, organizations for students with particular religious affiliations, and more. These organizations can help foster a sense of belonging for students, but they can also serve to advocate for student needs to ensure the college is inclusive and responding to their needs. Through clubs, students can develop their leadership skills by building a group and launching initiatives. The experiences of forming, leading, or contributing to a club can demonstrate to employers and graduate schools a level of collaboration and problem solving they may seek in candidates.

While students largely start and run these organizations, colleges can have an important role in their success. Colleges can provide support for these organizations and clubs, training for students who are leading them, and perhaps even some modest funding for them. Colleges can also foster collaboration and dialogue among and between groups, particularly to promote greater inclusion.

Students should seek out clubs that interest them or create one if one doesn't exist yet. Involvement fairs can help students find clubs, as the clubs are gathered in one common space. Colleges often curate directory lists of student organizations with updated contact information, which allows students to proactively reach out to organizations they wish to know more about. These can be especially helpful at large colleges, in which there can be hundreds of student clubs to choose from.

Given the power of peers to influence student behavior and academic performance, students should carefully assess clubs they are thinking of joining. Deciding how to allocate finite time in college is a central question, and if a single organization will demand much of a student's time outside of class, it's important to assess that seriously. The range of student and academic engagement opportunities in colleges, particularly in colleges that are excellent in student success, means that students should not feel pressured to join any given club in order to be successful in college. In other words, there is not any one club that is a prerequisite to student success. Moreover, clubs can uniquely allow students to try new hobbies or find new interests. Beyond student-run clubs, varsity sports at a college can cultivate immense fervor and pride among a student body. Importantly, not every club or activity has to be viewed only for its direct impact on a student's career. Enjoyment and play are also good for student success.

VOLUNTEERING AND COMMUNITY ENGAGEMENT

Volunteering and community engagement are important parts of students' development as citizens and learners. Volunteering can foster students' connection to their community, develop civic values, cultivate self-efficacy and leadership skills, and more (Mayhew et al., 2016). Through partnering with community organizations, initiatives, and individuals, students learn about complex, real-world issues and ways they may be addressed. Either through service-learning courses, as discussed in Chapter 5, or outside of the curriculum, colleges should provide some guidance and support for students to engage with community organizations. This can mean helping introduce students to challenges facing the community, the organizations working to address them, and ways to be involved.

The colleges most intentionally geared toward community engagement and student learning will do more than just provide opportunities for students to volunteer. These colleges are purposeful about fostering meaningful, mutually beneficial relationships between community organizations and students, as well as integrating volunteering into the curriculum and the college experience, helping students connect their learning with community challenges. Colleges will help students reflect, bringing students together to explore their thoughts on the issues addressed and pushing them to develop a more sophisticated understanding of the challenges facing communities.

The University of California–Riverside maintains a robust community service portal that offers training for students and allows them to search through community partner organizations and opportunities for volunteering, such as local schools in need of tutors, homeless shelters in need of fundraising support, and environmental organizations in need of people for a clean-up effort (University of California–Riverside, n.d.). The portal also showcases service events organized by the college, such as their large-scale Martin Luther King Day of Service and the Love Riverside Day of Service in which students partner with neighbors in the community to conduct beatification efforts across the city at schools, parks, and other sites.

Tulane University integrates community engagement throughout the student experience. The college has a public service graduation requirement, which asks all students to complete service-learning courses and conduct significant community service before they can graduate. Community service is embedded throughout the curriculum and the college's staff support student engagement in meaningful, collaborative partnerships with non-profit organizations across New Orleans and beyond (Tulane University, n.d.). For example, architecture students collaborated with a local non-profit organization in New Orleans in 2018 to build a new center and bike repair building. The students were guided through the experience by a Tulane professor and staff from the non-profit, helping students to analyze community needs, collaborate, and construct the project (Johns, 2018).

Overall, colleges can provide many different avenues for engagement with the community. These efforts, when done well, can have deep impacts on students and their experiences in college.

FRATERNITIES AND SORORITIES

Fraternities and sororities, which comprise what is known as "Greek life," are student organizations that build social communities among their members and maintain secret rites for membership. While there are academic-based, preprofessional (e.g., prelaw or premedicine) fraternities and sororities and organizations that use Greek letters in their names, here we primarily discuss the dominant model of social-based fraternity and sorority life.

Fraternities and sororities are relatively common in higher education, and their roles at colleges vary. Some colleges never had them or have dissolved them; at others, a majority of the student population is involved in different fraternities and sororities, significantly influencing student life at the college (*U.S. News & World Report,* 2020).

Fraternities and sororities initially developed at a time when racial segregation was commonplace. Greek life remains generally organized along gender and race dimensions. For the most part, members of fraternities identify as male and members of sororities identify as female. Some Greek life organizations are largely composed of people of a specific ethnic and racial background: a fraternity with students who are Black or a sorority with students of Hispanic origin, for instance.

These organizations can be very active, fostering community and lifelong friendships among their members. They can engage students in civic, philanthropic, and identity and leadership development activities (Mayhew et al., 2016). The organizations can also be springboards for involvement in other areas at the college.

While there can be benefits of joining a fraternity or sorority, it is important to evaluate these organizations, particularly because of how intensive they can be, how much time they can demand, and the power of peers to affect students' behavior, identity, and worldviews. Firstly, sororities and fraternities can be expensive. In order to be a member of these organizations, students are generally required to pay dues regularly, which may cost hundreds or thousands of dollars each time. Because fraternities and sororities often group people who are similar to each other together, students should be thoughtful about building a diverse peer network that encompasses their Greek organization and beyond. Students involved in fraternities or sororities, like all students, should be deliberate in undertaking experiences that challenge and prompt examination of their assumptions about themselves and the world around them. In short, students shouldn't rely on their Greek organizations alone to provide all their moral, social, and professional development.

Because these organizations are generally social in nature and ask significant time of their members, they can cut into the time a student spends in academic engagement. This can be particularly true during the academic term in which students join the fraternity or sorority in a process sometimes known as rushing or pledging. Researchers have found negative impacts on students' grade point averages during that term (Even & Smith, 2018). While some members of Greek life organizations believe that participation will increase their employment outcomes after college, these researchers also found no additional salary earnings because of an affiliation with a fraternity and sorority. Research has also found higher rates of academic cheating in fraternities and sororities (Mayhew et al., 2016). Finally, there have been significant challenges to these organizations over several years, particularly fraternities, as there are incidents of hazing, including deaths of students who are trying to pledge or join the organization, often involving alcohol intoxication or other substances.

Colleges have made efforts to promote student success for those involved with Greek life. Reforms at colleges have aimed to provide additional training and professional development for students in these organizations. Colleges also may regulate their social activities and new member pledging and onboarding processes. Other efforts have sought to increase transparency, making information about individual fraternities and sororities' academic performance, student conduct, activities, and accomplishments publicly visible. These kinds of efforts help students assess whether these organizations align with their desires and needs.

STUDENT GOVERNMENT

Student governments, through elected membership, form a representative organization for the student body at colleges. At some colleges, student governments are in charge of allocating funds to student organizations and other operations. Student government may also develop programming to enrich student life. At Georgia Tech, for example, their student government organized "Illuminate Tech," a free student speaker series in 2019 to discuss mental health on campus (Wyner, 2019).

Student governments are opportunities for students' civic development because they give students an opportunity to exercise and practice self-governance. Through elections, debate, legislative and executive and judicial processes, depending on the college, students can engage in the challenges and opportunities of democracy. Student government offers ample opportunity for leadership, providing highly developmental experiences that prepare students to participate more fully in community and public life. For students who are interested in pursuing a career in public service, having direct experience in college can transition well into the next chapter of their lives.

Regardless of what form student government takes at any given institution, the college should include students' voices in its operations, and student governments provide a vehicle to do that. A college committed to student success should regularly solicit students' feedback and involve students in the college's decisions where appropriate. Students should also be able to advocate for themselves and their issues, for which student government can be one avenue.

WHAT STUDENTS CAN DO BEFORE COLLEGE TO PREPARE

Before college, students can build familiarity with student clubs and organizations, joining and perhaps creating them while in high school. Many high schools also have their own forms of student government, even if they are more limited than what exists at the college level. Students in high school can model the intentional involvement in the community that many college students engage in by volunteering or doing community service work. Conceptually, high school students can start thinking early about how they want to spend their time and what social networks they want to develop.

College admissions officers, meanwhile, vary widely in their expectations for engagement of students during high school. Some may look specifically for engagement in clubs and organizations and community activities. Others may have more holistic assessments of students' engagement, including the commitments that some students may have to their family and helping them, perhaps working for a family business or taking care of a relative. The important task for the student, then, is to reflect, distill, and articulate the learning and growth that occurred during their time and how that supports their higher education goals.

> ### THREE GUIDING QUESTIONS TO ASK ABOUT STUDENT ENGAGEMENT AND LEADERSHIP DEVELOPMENT
>
> 1. To what extent does the college foster a sense of belonging throughout the institution?
> 2. To what extent does the college's culture and practices align with your ambitions and needs?
> 3. To what extent does the college have a wide range of student programming, clubs, and organizations—and the support for them—to engage and promote the development of their student population?

Table 6.1. A Rubric to Evaluate a College's Engagement and Leadership Development

Level	Indicators
Excellent	College sees life outside of courses as vital to student development and has purposeful, high-quality educational programming designed for the diversity of students; robust support for student organizations and other forms of student engagement is widespread; college provides excellent advising and programming for student community building and leadership development across the college experience.
Good	College's student life programming and guidance is generally high-quality; a widespread and diverse range of student organizations exists, with some training and leadership development for the students engaged; college has several efforts to foster community and engagement, but there are gaps in reaching the full student body.
Average	College's student life programming and guidance is of varied quality; college has a variety of student organizations and provides some support for them, but participation gaps remain; efforts to facilitate student belonging, community, and development exist, but do not reach segments of the student body.
Fair	College's student life programming and guidance is of highly variable quality; college has some student organizations and engagement activity, but limited programming and support to effectively engage the full student population.
Poor	College has little to no student organizations, student engagement programming, or community-building activity; there is a weak culture of student engagement; few efforts to foster an inclusive culture, sense of belonging, or guidance for student development and leadership exist.

CHAPTER 7

Mental Health, Safety, and Wellness

When Nicole began college, she was excited and ambitious, signing up to take a heavy course load. Even though most of her classes were intended for juniors or seniors, she was confident she could handle it. In high school, she had been high achieving, and she was used to doing well in her courses with little effort. As the weeks passed by, she began falling behind. It started with forgetting to do readings before class, which meant she didn't contribute in conversations. Nicole became so worried about not doing well on her essays that she would procrastinate, stay up all night in a mad dash to finish something, and turn in work she knew wasn't up to her standards. She stopped going to her professors' office hour appointments; she perceived her professors as being unhappy with her and panicked every time she thought about talking with them. More than anything, Nicole felt profoundly alone, and her depression and anxiety only worsened, and she considered dropping out of college entirely.

Many students struggle with mental health as they navigate college. In order for students to thrive in college, they need to feel safe and well. These conditions are basic to student success, and their absence can derail a student's academic journey, satisfaction with college, and sense of belonging (Eagan et al., 2014). Campuses around the country face challenges with respect to students' mental health, safety, and well-being. Colleges vary in their ability to adequately respond to these realities. In this chapter we explore the issues and how colleges respond to them, giving you practices to look for and consider when evaluating colleges.

COLLEGE STUDENTS' MENTAL HEALTH

Researchers have found that rates of depression, anxiety, hopelessness, suicidal thoughts, and other mental health issues are high among college students. Anxiety and depression are the most common reasons students are treated by mental health professionals, and the rates have climbed over time: The percentage of college students diagnosed with anxiety doubled from 10% in 2008 to 20% in 2018, and more than 60% of undergraduates reported feeling overwhelming anxiety at some time within the previous 12 months (American College Health Association [ACHA], 2018; Sutton, 2019). In fact, in 2018 around 10% of college students reported seriously considering suicide (ACHA, 2018). High rates have been found across the student populations, but racial, ethnic, sexual, or gender minorities are especially vulnerable, with two-thirds of transgender students and half of bisexual students reporting self-injury in a 2018 study (Liu et al., 2018).

Stressful life events contribute to these high rates of mental health challenges. College students must navigate new environments, expectations, and relationships, all the while operating outside of the support and familiar structures they may have had before college. While some challenges and stressful events are expected and can be formative for students, like a test or presentation, others can be detrimental, depending on how students make meaning and respond to these experiences. Students are reporting that they are having experiences that are traumatic or difficult to handle: academic struggles, estrangement from loved ones, economic anxiety, discrimination, world events outside of their control, and more. These challenges are associated with increased mental health diagnoses, self-harm, and suicidality (Becker, 2020; Bethune, 2019).

Students also arrive at college with preexisting medical and mental health histories. In fact, of the college students who contemplate suicide, about 80% of them had already thought about suicide during high school (Brownson et al., 2016). Students are also coming to colleges with childhood experiences that make them more vulnerable to the stress of college, such as a death of a family member, physical or emotional abuse, homelessness, and parental divorce (Resilience Project, 2018).

There have been great strides in the United States and beyond in reducing stigma around mental health, increasing access to treatment, and empowering people to seek mental health support. Ben Locke, director of the Center for Collegiate Mental Health based at Penn State University, describes this shift: "We have been decreasing negative judgments of people around mental health. . . . The students who are coming to college grew up in an era where talking about distress is normal" (Locke, cited in Woolf, 2019).

Colleges have become providers of mental health and related services. In 2019, counseling centers at colleges in the United States saw an average of about 12% of students at a college (Brown, 2020). Done well, counseling can have positive outcomes, not only helping students stay enrolled in college, but also helping them develop new and healthier ways of thinking and being in the world (Downs et al., 2018). Institutions, however, vary greatly in their approaches and in how well they meet the needs of students. At some colleges, students have to wait weeks to get an initial appointment for therapy. To evaluate a college's mental health infrastructure, we can ask many questions. For treatment and management of mental health challenges, does the college have a counseling center? How well is it staffed? And by whom? Are they professionally trained at high levels? Are there wait times? Many campuses report long waits, sometimes weeks, for students to get an appointment (Thielking, 2017). But if you are in crisis or need to talk to someone, that kind of wait can be dangerous. Colleges should at least have walk-in appointment availability where students can be seen, at least for a first evaluation.

And once students do get in, how many counseling sessions can they get? Many institutions struggle to meet the needs of students. At colleges where therapists have high caseloads, students may be seen for therapy only every 3 to 4 weeks, or they may receive no continuing care at all after an initial session (Brown, 2020). These workloads make therapists less effective—that is, students show less improvement in their symptoms of anxiety, depression, and distress (Brown, 2020).

As you examine colleges' mental health services, there are different things you can look for. The Center for Collegiate Mental Health recommends that caseloads for each therapist be no more than 150 students; after about 150 students they see declines in the quality of services (Brown, 2020). Therefore, you should ask a college's counseling services how many students each therapist sees. In addition, some colleges may have additional costs for services, or counseling may be included in the students' fees with no additional costs to students. And beyond the campus counseling center, does the college have a referral network to community mental health providers for continued care or more specialized care? Another consideration is if mental health services are only available for students that attend college in-person, or if there is a way for remote or online students to access them too.

PREVENTATIVE PRACTICES IN MENTAL HEALTH

Colleges can help prevent or mitigate mental health challenges among students. These efforts can include, among other things, training for professors, staff, and students on recognizing symptoms of distress and how to direct others to appropriate resources (Becker, 2020). There are also more formal systems of reporting and monitoring students of concern. To facilitate a culture in which people say something when they see something that is concerning, many colleges have platforms through which students and others can alert the appropriate personnel at the college of concerning behavior or an incident.

Additionally, colleges can help reduce students' feelings of isolation or lack of connection to a community. When students feel isolated, they have lower rates of psychological well-being. Community-building programming can increase students' social connection and engage them in activities that strengthen students' sense of belonging. The peer learning communities discussed in Chapter 6 are one such effort. Finally, healthy lifestyles among students can be promoted through educational campaigns and student clubs centered around well-being. Because high rates of illicit drug and alcohol use contribute to the downward performance of students, colleges use these campaigns, clubs, and other programs to reduce alcohol and substance use (Martin, 2019).

One example of a robust culture and proactive program is the University of Vermont Wellness Environment, which is a comprehensive residential, curricular, and co-curricular initiative that encourages wellness thinking and behaviors among students (University of Vermont, n.d.). Another is Florida State University's Student Resilience Project, which asks all students who enter the college to go through a series of online modules that build students' resilience, helping students understand and normalize the stressors and challenges of higher education and how students can respond to them. The project empowers students with psychosocial tools, such as stress management, journaling, and mindfulness techniques that they can use as they progress through college (Resilience Project, 2018).

Resources like these help students change their perceptions of challenges: What they might view as permanent signs that college is not for them become temporary obstacles that can be overcome. Paul Tough (2014) writes in the *New York Times Magazine* about how these interventions can help shift students' paradigms:

> Sure, [students] still feel bad when they fail a test or get in a fight with a roommate or are turned down for a date. But in general, they don't interpret those setbacks as a sign that they don't belong in college or that they're not going to succeed there. (n.p.)

A college that doesn't have robust and proactive activities for student mental health can experience dire consequences. A student at a college without such an approach could end up leaving higher education altogether without much intervention from the college at all. At a college with better mental health resources, a student's symptoms could be quickly noticed when they stopped attending a course. This student could be connected to their college's resources and receive the help they need.

Take the case of Joanne, a college junior. Her first 2 years at college were relatively easy; she did well in her classes and made a fair number of friends. The summer after her sophomore year, though, her friends began to drift away. She entered the fall term feeling lonely. Her classes were harder than she'd expected. At the beginning of the semester, she spent time studying, but as her feelings of loneliness intensified, she felt less and less motivated. She began skipping class, and rarely left her off-campus apartment. As her grades started dropping, she felt that there was nothing she could do to salvage her grades and that there was no point in trying. Seven weeks into the semester, she received an email from one of her professors. The professor explained that he'd noticed Joanne's absence in class and was concerned. Given the invitation to talk about what had been going on, Joanne opened up about her struggles. She was connected to counseling services at her college that provided professional help and was able to work with the professor to get back on track in the course.

CASE MANAGEMENT

Most colleges have services, in the form of case management or associated personnel, to handle instances of students dealing with major accidents, illnesses, and other issues. These services are also known as student support centers or student care programs at different colleges. These staff members can connect students to services and resources on campus and in the community. They can also help students if they need to withdraw from college for a term or need other accommodations, and they advocate for students as needed. They can work directly with professors to accommodate students' needs with exams, assignments, and other deadlines.

When Benjamin first learned about case management, he'd assumed that it was not for students like him. He had no serious issues with his health or wellness. However, in the middle of the semester, he got into a serious car accident. As he tried to cope with his recovery, transportation, and medical bills, he felt increasingly overwhelmed. He struggled to complete assignments on time and realized that his grades were slipping. After he missed yet another deadline, Benjamin realized he needed help. He reached out to case management and met with a staff member the following week. The case manager helped him navigate communicating with his instructors, obtain extensions for his work, and develop strategies for managing his stress. Without this service, Benjamin would have had no avenue for formal assistance as he dealt with a short-term crisis.

FAMILY, GUARDIANS, AND STUDENT WELL-BEING

Family members and guardians play a role in student well-being across their educational journey. Research has found that emotional support from families is associated with a lift to students' grades, but emotional support can do so much more (Roksa & Kinsley, 2018). It is also associated with an improved sense of belonging and student engagement in college, including how students engage with professors, how much they study, and their feelings of belonging (Roksa & Kinsley, 2018).

Family members can also watch for signs of mental health challenges in their child, complementing the mental health interventions and resources existing at a college. Families can contact the college or police directly if they are worried about their students. Officials can try and reach the student, and, if necessary, conduct a welfare check, in which the student is visited and their condition assessed. From there, the student can be connected to appropriate resources and the family can be updated on the student's well-being.

That said, overparenting, also known as helicopter parenting, sees parents "excessively monitor their children and often remove obstacles from their paths, instead of helping them develop the skills to handle the inevitable difficulties of life" (Wellock, 2019). Because students' opportunities for growth are stifled, this style of parenting can negatively impact students during college and interfere with a healthy developmental trajectory in which students assume and manage more adult responsibilities. Overparenting can undermine both a student's sense of autonomy and self-confidence (Bradley-Geist & Olson-Buchanan, 2014; Schiffrin et al., 2013). In studies examining the relationships between parenting and college, students who reported having overcontrolling and overinvolved parents reported higher levels of depression, stress, and burnout with school, and less satisfaction with life (Love et al., 2019).

SAFETY AND POLICING

Colleges typically have their own police and security forces that are charged with promoting a safe campus and place to learn, in concert with the college's administration. College police forces may respond to on-campus incidents more quickly than the local police. Additionally, campus police are able to offer campus-specific services that might not be otherwise available (Reaves, 2015). And at many colleges, campus police have similar powers to traditional municipal police forces, so they can conduct investigations and make arrests as necessary.

So how can colleges promote greater safety? What are some signs of a responsible approach to student safety to look for at a college? A good place to start evaluating how a college approaches student safety is to ask current students at the college questions about how they perceive their safety. If there are particular concerns, a student may want to ask targeted questions or reach out to the president of a student group of interest, such as a club for students who are LGBTQ+.

To gain further insight, one can examine the college's police force itself. Campus police forces vary widely across higher education, with different levels of sophistication, approaches, and resources. It's important to consider if the campus police force has enough personnel to meet the needs of the college and its students, and if they operate effectively. Key characteristics to look out for are the responsiveness and promptness of the police force. If there is ever an incident that elevates students' risk, like an active shooter or a bad car accident, these qualities are crucial.

A national study of campus police forces found that the average officer-to-student ratio was 2.4 officers per 1,000 students (Reaves, 2015). However, this ratio alone isn't enough to determine the level of support offered by police; factors such as the size and location of the campus, technology, hours of teaching, and public safety needs can all complicate how meaningful this ratio is (Woolfenden & Stevenson, 2011). Another marker might be to see if the campus police force is accredited by a state, national, or international body that accredits campus police forces to ensure high standards of operation and best practices. The University of Delaware's police force, for example, is accredited through the Commission on Accreditation for Law Enforcement Agencies and the International Association of Campus Law Enforcement Administrators (University of Delaware Police Department, n.d.).

Many campuses, if not most, also have emergency blue light communication systems throughout the campus. These are emergency poles with lights and remote communication systems to the police. If a person on campus is in trouble or has an emergency, they can use the blue light systems to talk with the police or other emergency responder. Since the poles are illuminated and may flash when activated, they can help direct first responders to the scene. However, some campuses do not have blue light communication systems and use another approach instead. No rigorous research has been done to determine which of the emergency systems in use among college campuses results in greatest safety for students, but clearly these blue light systems serve as symbols of safety and are convenient for students.

Campuses can take more preventative approaches to physical and public safety. Colleges should regularly assess their campus to determine if there are areas that are dangerous, poorly illuminated, or could be threats to safety. The college should then make modifications based on the results. Student residence halls may have automatic lock systems so that the door is always locked and students need some kind of identity verification to securely access the building. Campuses may also offer self-defense courses, as well as active shooter training sessions, to help students and staff members know how to best respond to these situations.

When a student is sexually assaulted, it can compromise their time in higher education and have lifelong impacts (Potter et al., 2018). Women in college are three times more likely than women not in college to experience sexual violence (Sinozich & Langton, 2014). In response, colleges have developed and expanded sexual violence prevention efforts that aim to shift culture, educate about sexual consent, and reduce risk behavior. The University of Oregon, for instance, has a multifaceted sexual violence prevention effort, including student trainings, student groups focused on the issue, and an alliance of professionals and students across campus that includes representatives from the police department, college health center, and more (University of Oregon, n.d.).

Many colleges also have robust investigatory and adjudication procedures for student cases of misconduct. For criminal acts, these will go through police proceedings. Students may also face campus conduct hearings in which fellow students or administrators weigh in on how to respond. Should the student be expelled, suspended, engage in ethics training and reflection, or have some other consequences? These sorts of hearings can also happen after students are suspected of cheating or plagiarizing.

Finally, colleges vary widely in their approaches to transporting students. While many colleges rely on students bringing cars, motorcycles, or other forms of transportation to college, this may not be common at more urban or smaller campuses. Regardless, inadequate means of getting to and around campus can create safety and logistical concerns, especially at night, during peak times, or if a student has impaired mobility. Some colleges offer discounted ride services via taxi or a ride hailing app service for students to use if they feel unsafe or are unable to drive safely. A college's location, busing system, transportation, accessibility, and parking can have important implications for students' daily lives in college.

FOOD AND DINING

Food is fundamental to student success. If you aren't eating well, it's hard to do well in college. Many college campuses have several food and dining options. Some even have mandatory meal plans. It can be easy to fall into stereotypes of college students eating pizza or fast food all day and not eating in healthy ways. But a healthy diet is important for maintaining a student's physical and mental well-being—and for academic performance. The college, then, should give attention to the food it offers, ensuring there are healthy options for students and encouragement to consume them. When assessing colleges, evaluate what options are available in the dining halls and how they match your dietary needs, such as vegetarian/vegan, allergies, or religious accommodations.

But eating meals is about more than sustenance. Eating with other college community members is also part of the educational ecosystem, helping students build friendships with peers from inside and outside of their courses. Colleges with many students living on campus may particularly value college dining halls as venues for substantive intellectual discussion and development.

Some critics dismiss concerns around student dining options as being frivolous or, worse yet, a sign of students being overly coddled. But a reality is that students care about what they will be eating, and many have deeper reasons for that care. Consider, for example, Leah, a student who is Jewish. She lived on campus her first year and used her college dining plan for all her meals. Leah observed Passover, a Jewish holiday in which Jews do not eat anything with yeast in it. She was dismayed to find that there were no food options available for her, as the dining staff could not provide meals that adhered to her religious dietary needs. Leah spent most of that week hungry; her budget allowed for few options outside of the meal plan she had paid for, and there was no Jewish Student Union to fill the gap. More than the inconvenience of the week, though, Leah's experience made her question if the college truly welcomed people like her. She no longer felt that the college fostered an inclusive environment and was skeptical of its claims toward fostering diversity.

Will, a student who is vegan, also lived on campus his first year. However, he chose not to purchase a meal plan, knowing that there would be few vegan food options for him. Unlike Leah, he was prepared to purchase groceries and cook on his own. However, he hadn't considered the social element of eating. When his roommate and people from his residence hall went to eat together at the dining hall between classes, Will had to rush back to his room to make sure he had something substantial to eat. A few times he had tried going with his friends and eating what he could, but he found that he was hungry during class and had trouble paying attention. As he ate more of his meals away from his friends, Will found that he felt like he was missing inside jokes, or that plans for the weekend were made without him. Without being able to take part in the communal environment of meals, Will felt increasingly socially isolated.

Meeting students' food needs is complicated, connected with financial aid but also with public services and community programs. Many college students suffer from food insecurity, in which they do not have reliable access to food options (Goldrick-Rab et al., 2019). Housing insecurity can compound problems related to accessing food. These inequalities can also affect students' connection and self-perception. For instance, being able to afford to eat in a college dining hall, particularly on a meal plan, can be seen as a luxury by some students who cannot afford it, creating separation between student populations and potentially affecting students' sense of belonging at the campus. Colleges can offer supplemental financial aid to cover food and housing expenses and offer and destigmatize a food pantry for students. They can also work proactively with students and community agencies to ensure basic needs are met.

CAMPUS HEALTHCARE

What do students do when they are sick? Most colleges where students are living on campus have student health centers where providers see students for a host of medical issues. These centers vary in quality, range of services, and facilities. College health centers also typically work with professors and employers, providing notes and evidence that a student had to miss class or work due to sickness.

Some colleges include health insurance requirements for all their students; that is, you either buy the college's insurance plan or demonstrate that you already have equivalent health insurance. Health insurance requirements add costs to college, but they can also be critically important to students, who can obtain necessary care without incurring medical debt that could otherwise derail their college career and their credit score. Even though many students do not think they will need it, having convenient access to high-quality and affordable healthcare is crucial. This is especially true if a student has serious or chronic health issues.

As you look at the campus healthcare options at any given college, here are some important considerations. As mentioned above, many colleges have health centers, but others also may have hospitals and specialized services, such as support for students who are recovering from an addiction. You'll want to consider the capacity of the health facility to meet students' needs. Particular considerations include how long the wait times are, the quality of care, and the different services a health center provides. If no health center or hospital exists on campus, students may be directed to find a provider in the community. If this is the case, you'll want to pay special attention to what assistance the college gives in finding providers.

RECREATION AND PERSONAL FITNESS

Part of wellness is recreation and personal fitness. Many colleges have invested in robust facilities and programming to engage students in physical activities. These activities help promote student health during their college years, and they also cultivate habits for good health over students' lifetimes.

Recreation centers and gyms provide convenient places for students, particularly those who are living on campus, to exercise. Many campus recreation centers will provide equipment for students to exercise individually. Others may host group fitness classes or sessions. One consideration is the capacity of the recreation center: Is it possible for students to easily access the form of exercise they enjoy? Or is the recreation center always very crowded?

Campuses may also have intramural sports. These competitions allow students within the college to form teams and compete in various sports, such as kickball, basketball, or volleyball. Intramural sports can engage students and build community. The evidence suggests that participation can have positive impacts on academic performance and student success, helping promote community, sense of belonging, and health, so long as participation is balanced with academic needs (Vasold et al., 2019).

SPIRITUAL WELLNESS

Spiritual wellness is another dimension of student wellness that can play an important role in many students' lives. Students come to college with various religious views. Without the same level of familial involvement and removed from their home environment, college is often a time in which students reevaluate held religious and spiritual assumptions. Colleges should be sensitive to these changes and to many students' desires to continue to practice and evolve their religious identities.

Colleges can support students' spirituality by establishing cultural norms that foster intentional connection and discussion. Student organizations that bring people together of similar faiths provide another source of community and belonging for spiritual students. Colleges can also coordinate and partner with religious groups, such as campus ministries, to facilitate student activity, growth, and common programming. If your religious faith or tradition is something that you want to integrate into your college experience, you will want to make sure that you can feel comfortable practicing it in the prospective college and its community. One area of opportunity for student learning and wellness is interfaith efforts at colleges. Research has found that intentional engagement with other faiths can foster positive appreciation and understanding of diverse others and worldviews (Elfman, 2019). This can take the form of attending religious services of other traditions, engaging in informal conversations, or an interfaith student retreat. In fact, researchers have found that having a friendship with a person of another faith improved students' appreciation of that faith (Interfaith Youth Core, 2019). Even more, there are long-term positive impacts in how students develop attitudes toward others with various worldviews, helping students become more accepting and appreciative of the diversity of ways of being in the world—increasingly important attitudes as graduates enter diverse workplaces and communities around the world. An example of interfaith work in higher education is that of Interfaith Youth Core, a Chicago-based nonprofit that brings college students of various faiths together through community service and dialogue. Another example is the University Interfaith Council at the University of California–Santa Cruz, which brings together people of different faiths to foster shared dialogue, share spiritual perspectives on educational programs, and celebrate the variety of religious identities at the college (University Interfaith Council, n.d.).

WHAT STUDENTS CAN DO BEFORE COLLEGE TO PREPARE

Students can make intentional efforts to establish health and wellness practices and habits surrounding physical and mental health before college. Because the college application itself can add significant stress to students and upend habits and practices, it can be a good time to be purposeful in cultivating them. Some practices that can help students build resilience are practicing self-care, developing realistic goals, keeping organized, and building connections and relationships with others (American Psychological Association, 2020). Part of keeping organized is managing your time: using a calendar, assigning set times to study, and so on.

Students can also develop health and wellness transition plans from high school to college, particularly if they are moving to a new location for college. This can include establishing new healthcare providers, wellness opportunities, and other specialty needs that a student may have for their healthcare in their new community. This transition plan can include conversations with family members and guardians about boundaries and communication when the student goes to college. These boundaries should give the student agency to grow on their own while still providing familial support for guidance and assistance when needed.

THREE GUIDING QUESTIONS TO ASK ABOUT MENTAL HEALTH, SAFETY, AND WELLNESS

1. To what extent does the institution have sufficient capacity and high-quality staff to support student safety and wellness?
2. To what extent does the institution take a holistic approach to fostering well-being, including preventative practices and cultivating healthy habits among students?
3. To what extent does the college have support and safety nets in place for students who encounter particular challenges or hardships?

Table 7.1. A Rubric for Evaluating a College's Approach to Student Wellness

Level	Indicators
Excellent	College has a full and robust culture of well-being, with high-quality programming to support holistic physical and mental wellness, including prevention; college has adequate facilities, staffing, and resources to meet the diverse needs of its students; college has robust safety and security operations; students report feeling safe.
Good	College has many health and wellness services and prevention programming that are generally of high quality; efforts reach much but not all of the student body; police and safety measures are proactive and widespread and students generally report feeling safe.
Average	College has services for mental and physical healthcare, with staffing and resources that often don't meet student demand; prevention efforts to bolster physical and mental wellness are present, but their reach isn't across the entire student body, with significant gaps; police and safety measures are present, but there are students who report not feeling safe.
Fair	College has basic student wellness efforts, but they are understaffed and underresourced; college has limited prevention efforts; college safety and security efforts are present, but similarly understaffed, with some students feeling unsafe.
Poor	College has little support for student wellness; students are generally left on their own to find and secure care and support when needed; little to no prevention efforts exist; security and safety measures are limited, with many students falling through the cracks and not feeling safe.

Part IV

FUNDING AND LAUNCHING FROM COLLEGE

CHAPTER 8

Money Matters

Costs and Financial Aid

Harrison, a recent high school graduate, was working two jobs over the summer to save money before college started in the fall. A few weeks before the semester started, he sat down at his kitchen table to make sure his budget was in order. The costs of college kept adding up: expensive textbooks, a special calculator for his math classes, undisclosed technology fees, and more. On top of that, he knew that tuition itself would be due soon. Looking at his list of expenses, Harrison was frustrated and stressed. He didn't feel like his college was transparent about all the little things that would cost him money, and when he called the financial aid office, he was put on hold for over an hour. When he finally did speak to someone, they weren't helpful and seemed harried. He hung up the phone feeling more overwhelmed than ever. As the semester grew closer and closer to beginning, Harrison was stuck with the same list of expenses and the same feeling of stress he'd had a few weeks ago.

College can be expensive, and these costs can be an impediment to success for many students. From 1989–90 to 2019–20, average tuition and fees tripled at public colleges in the United States and doubled at private colleges, after adjusting for inflation (College Board, 2019). The average tuition and fees at public colleges was over $10,000 per year, and over $36,000 at private colleges, in the 2019–2020 academic year. And tuition isn't the only cost students have while in college; there are costs for housing, food, books, and other out-of-class experiences. All in, as of 2020, several private colleges cost around $300,000 for 4 years, with continued increases expected each year. All of these increases might be palatable if financial aid had increased proportionally with the rising costs of attending college, but it hasn't. Median family income has not kept pace with the increases either, making it harder for many students and families to afford higher education (College Board, 2019).

Students' challenges in paying for college contributes to significant gaps in students, particularly those from a low-income background, going to college and succeeding there (Harnisch & Lebioda, 2016). The costs have also contributed to increased student loan debt in the United States, with around $1.6 trillion of debt in 2019, exceeding the size of credit card debt in America. On average, about 7 in 10 students graduate from college with debt, owing around $30,000 per borrower as of 2019 (Institute for College Access & Success, 2019). And not everyone can pay their loans back; the average default rate on student loan debt was around 10% in 2016 (U.S. Department of Education, 2019). The debt students incur for college can also impact students as they launch from college, affecting graduates' jobs options and financial ability to participate in life's other major financial hurdles, like buying a house or saving for retirement.

Given these economic trends, it's easy to see why people are nervous about the expense of higher education. What will the long-term impacts of the cost be? Does a more expensive college mean higher quality? How much is too much, and how should costs and other expenses be evaluated?

UNDERSTANDING THE COSTS OF COLLEGE

When we hear people say that college costs a lot, it's often unclear where the cost comes from. What exactly are the things that make it so expensive?

Colleges are tasked with presenting students a cost of attendance figure. This sum represents the total costs to attend the institution each year. The cost of attendance guides not only students' attendance decisions, but colleges' financial aid award decisions.

Let's say a college lists its total costs of attendance as $26,000 per year. How did they arrive at that figure? There are several component parts:

- *Tuition ($11,000):* This is the cost for the courses you enroll in. Students can be charged per course/credit hour, or as a block charge allowing them to register for up to a certain number of courses in an academic term.
- *Fees ($2,000):* Fees are typically smaller sums of money than tuition, and can include things like parking fees, recreation fees, financial aid fees, student activities fees, or online course fees.

- **Books and Supplies ($1,000):** This is the average costs of the textbooks and any other course materials required to attend a college full time. Some majors may require additional supplies. Students in a nursing program may need scrubs, while a biology major may need special lab equipment, for instance. Students may also be able to borrow free textbooks or other materials from the college library. Some bookstores will allow students to rent textbooks and return them at the end of the academic term.
- **Transportation ($1,000):** This is the estimated cost of getting to and from campus.
- **Housing and Food ($9,000):** This is the average cost to live and eat at the college or in the city where the college is located.
- **Miscellaneous Personal Expenses ($2,000):** This is the estimated amount for other day-to-day costs, like clothing, laundry, and entertainment.

The costs of attendance across different colleges vary. Some public institutions have a cost of attendance closer to $20,000 per year, while some private colleges have tuition costs around $60,000 per year and costs of attendance that are nearly $80,000 per year. Further, as we'll explore later in the chapter, with different forms of financial aid, many students do not actually pay the full cost of attendance that is listed on a college's website. Given the ranges in price and costs, and the aid that is provided to students, a more detailed evaluation of the full costs of a college, and all that it might entail, is critical to assessing the potential for the investment. Moreover, it is important to realize the actual cost for an individual student to attend a college may vary greatly beyond a college's official cost of attendance.

First, there are significant variations in costs depending on students' lifestyles. A student may spend more on a luxury apartment, or on high-cost social activities, such as eating out. There may be peer pressure to spend significant amounts on these kinds of lifestyle amenities. While there can be a place for these activities in students' lives, they can also be very expensive without clearly contributing to the student's success or educational growth. If a student is from out of state, transportation costs for returning home may increase their overall expenses.

Second, students often participate in enrichment programs and opportunities that are generally not included in the cost of attendance calculations. Studying abroad and internships, for instance, may add significant additional expenses to college; a summer term studying abroad could cost $10,000, $20,000, or more, depending on the college. An unpaid summer internship could have several thousand dollars in costs in travel and housing, not including any lost income that a student may incur by not working in paid employment during that summer internship. Given the importance of participating in these kinds of applied and experiential learning activities, as discussed in Chapter 5, students and their families who have financial need should look for what kind of support from the college is available to enable their participation.

A common assumption is that the most expensive college is inherently the best. Is this true? Do you get what you pay for? No, not exactly.

First, students and their families may not actually see the full cost to educate a student in a college's tuition price. A low tuition that the student pays does not necessarily indicate the college's full cost of educating the student, which may be much higher. Public colleges are generally cheaper than private colleges because some of their expenses are covered by the government, helping to reduce the costs to students and their families. That said, there can be significant variations in the level of state support given to public colleges, which can impact the price of tuition. Meanwhile, private colleges generally do not have financial support from the government to subsidize tuition. As a result, they must ask students and their families to pay for much of the cost of their education. Private colleges, however, frequently offer discounts or significant financial aid to reduce the actual costs students pay, which may make private colleges more accessible.

Second, colleges' funds may be spent on things that do not bolster student success. While it's true that having more money gives colleges the ability to invest in resources that bolster student learning and growth, not all colleges spend money equally well. Some colleges may spend more money than others on inefficient operations or marketing or other expenses where there isn't a clear return for students. Others may spend money on things that have promise to elevate student success but aren't delivered effectively. It's possible a college may hire an additional instructor to address gaps in student performance in a major, for instance, but that instructor may not be a strong teacher—and if the college lacks professional development for its faculty, the instructor may not use the kinds of evidence-based teaching approaches discussed in Chapter 3 that lift the learning of all students.

While it is tempting, particularly for students from lower-income families, to go to the college that is the cheapest, this may not reflect the best value. Costs and aid must be examined in the context of overall quality and a student's likelihood of having success at a college, which, as we have seen, is dependent on many factors. For instance, attending a low-cost college where the majority of students don't graduate or where most students graduate in 6 years, not 4, can be costly. Researchers estimate that once you factor in college expenses and lost wages over the lifespan, an extra year in college on average costs more than $85,000, and 2 extra years cost about $174,000 (Abel & Deitz, 2014). In other words, it may seem like you are saving in the short term by prioritizing low costs, but doing so may significantly increase the risk of not graduating, having a delayed graduation, or not developing the dispositions and skills that employers want and that will yield a fruitful career. As the U.S. Department of Education (2015) writes:

> The most expensive education is one that doesn't lead to a degree. While graduating with high levels of debt is holding too many [students] back from reaching their full potential, the even more damaging outcome is for students who take on debt but never complete their degree. In fact, students' ability to repay their loans depends more strongly on whether they graduate than on how much total debt they take on.

RETURN ON INVESTMENT IN HIGHER EDUCATION

While college is one of the most significant expenses in a person's life, a degree still represents one of the best investments a person can make in their life. Graduates with a college degree earn about $1 million more over their lifetime than if they had just a high school diploma (Carnevale et al., 2015). Graduates are also more likely to be employed. Research shows that college graduates have half the unemployment rate of those with just a high school degree and are far more likely to be in high-earning positions (Ma et al., 2019).

Moreover, a college degree increases the chance that a person will move up the socioeconomic ladder. In fact, researchers have found that for the typical 4-year college graduate, the return on investment is so pronounced that the returns can cover the full costs of college in a little over a decade after graduating (Ma et al., 2019). Beyond these financial returns, there are a myriad of other benefits associated with obtaining a college education. A college education is associated with healthier lifestyles, longer lives, increased voting and volunteering, and more (Ma et al., 2019).

Keeping in mind these data-supported benefits, it's still important to make financially wise decisions along the higher education journey, and to do so in a way that increases return on investment. Below we explore some of the major financial decisions people have to make during higher education and how we should think about them in the context of student success.

WHAT IS FINANCIAL AID?

Most students in college do not have enough money from their families or other personal savings to pay for their time in college. As a result, many turn to financial aid. Financial aid, at its core, is the money that is allocated to a student to support the costs to attend college.

In order to qualify for many kinds of aid, students must complete what is known as the FAFSA: The Free Application for Federal Student Aid, which is managed by the U.S. Department of Education. Students enter all sorts of information on this form about their incomes, families, and expenses. From there, the federal government calculates each student's Expected Family Contribution (EFC), which is what the government would expect the student's family to contribute to the student's college expenses.

For the lowest-income families, the EFC is zero—the federal government doesn't expect the family to have any resources available to help the student pay for college. For higher-income families, the federal government may calculate that the family has the ability to contribute significantly to a student's education each year, perhaps at levels over one hundred thousand dollars a year. The data from the FAFSA is then sent to each college the student indicates on the form. Once received, the college takes its costs of attendance figure (how much it costs to attend the school for a year), subtracts the EFC figure (what the family should pay), and the remaining amount determines the financial need of each student. From there, the college can determine what kind of financial aid a student might be eligible for, if any.

Unfortunately, many students with financial need don't even fill the FAFSA out, leaving on the table money that would improve their lives. Too often, this is because of a lack of information or confusion over the process. The FAFSA completion rate is very low among students from some states, such as Utah, where the completion rate in 2018 was only about 35% (Heath, 2018). These low rates are why some states, like Texas, have started to require all graduating high school seniors to fill out the FAFSA.

In addition to the FAFSA, there may be separate scholarship and grant applications at each college, as well as scholarships from local community-based organizations, foundations, and college alumni groups. Many private colleges ask students to complete the College Board's College Scholarship Service Profile (CSS Profile). The data from the CSS Profile is used to determine financial aid from the college itself.

WHAT ARE THE DIFFERENT FORMS OF FINANCIAL AID?

Grants

Grants are sums of money that are typically awarded to students with financial need. Grants, unlike loans, do not need to be repaid, and have been shown to improve students' ability to attend and graduate from college in a timely manner (Denning et al., 2019; Page & Scott-Clayton, 2016). They are mostly funded by federal and state governments but can also be awarded by institutions. Grants that are based on a student's financial need are evaluated each year to ensure a student's financial situation has not changed such that they no longer qualify, like if a parent received a large salary increase.

At the federal level, the Pell Grant is the largest and most well-known, supporting students from lower-income backgrounds. In 2018–2019, the maximum Pell Grant was just over $6,000. Not every family's income qualifies them for the full amount; the average grant in 2018–2019 was $4,160. Nearly half of the recipients' families had incomes at or below $20,000 (College Board, 2019). Individual states may have other need-based grant programs that can supplement the federal government's Pell Grant, such as California's Cal Grant program, which provides funding for lower-income college students.

Scholarships

Scholarships, like grants, are a form of funding that does not need to be repaid, and some may be used for college expenses beyond tuition. Scholarships can be provided by a state government, college, or other organizations. Merit scholarships, the most common form, are awarded by criteria of achievement, like GPA or SAT scores, and often do not factor in a student's financial need. There are also hybrid scholarships that are both need- and merit-sensitive. That is, the scholarship may have certain merit criteria, such as a high GPA, but also have a need-based component.

Scholarships that are awarded based on a student's merit are primarily designed to attract a student to enroll at a particular college. One common aim of state government merit scholarship programs is to keep students within the state for college—thereby keeping the students' talent and their future employment more likely to stay in the state's economy. Examples of such programs are Florida's Bright Futures or Georgia's HOPE Scholarships.

Despite their wide appeal, merit scholarships have been criticized. A common eligibility criterion is standardized test scores. Higher scores on the SAT, for example, have been correlated to income, with students from higher-income families obtaining higher scores. As a result, merit-based programs tend to go to students from families of mid-level incomes or above. Some claim that merit-based programs are thus unfair, awarding funds to wealthier families while many lower-income students may not receive much-needed financial assistance.

Work Study

Work-study programs are for students with financial need, and are typically funded by the federal government, the state, or the individual college. Work-study is primarily a funding source for students to be employed in on-campus jobs, such as helping with clerical tasks, assisting in research or teaching, tutoring other students, or helping operate the library or an administrative office. In some cases, work-study funding is used to employ students in community organizations like non-profits or even in private companies. Research shows that work-study programs can benefit students beyond the financial component. Participating students may have access to better jobs, spend less time commuting, and have more flexibility in their schedule. Importantly, work-study programs can offer a stronger connection to students' academic goals than a traditional job (Scott-Clayton & Minaya, 2016).

Too often, however, work-study programs do not live up to their full potential to impact student growth or development. Unfulfilling work-study programs may have students sit at desks without much actual work, supervision, guided reflection, or connections to students' educational or career goals. Implemented properly, work-study can be much more than just a means for financial aid. Work-study can have a positive impact on student success, increasing on-campus engagement and the likelihood of a student graduating and launching successfully after graduation (Mayhew et al., 2016).

Income-Share Agreements

While not especially common, students do take out what are called income-share agreements. In these agreements, an individual, college, or other organization agrees to fund a student's studies, and, in return, the student agrees to pay a fixed portion of their salary after graduating for a certain number of years. A student might agree to pay 10% of their salary for 10 years, for example.

Purdue University created its Income Share Agreement program in 2019 as an alternative to private bank loans or other loans with high interest rates. Purdue caps the amount to be repaid at 2.5 times the amount the student borrowed (Mumford, 2020). Because students may end up paying much more than they borrowed in income-share agreements, they should be approached with caution. A student should generally consider these types of agreements only if other forms of public aid, such as federal student loans, have been exhausted.

Waivers and Tuition Discounts

Many colleges offer significant waivers and discounting of tuition rates for students. Many public colleges, for instance, will waive the out-of-state tuition to attract students of high merit. That is, if a public college asks $26,000 for out-of-state tuition but $9,000 for in-state students, the college may offer a 100% waiver of the out-of-state portion of tuition, bringing the student's tuition to the in-state rate. A private college may have other discounting mechanisms to reduce tuition rates for students. Students may qualify for these if they are the child of a graduate of the college, have unmet financial need, or have special circumstances—or if the college is simply trying to enroll more students.

Emergency Aid and Completion Grants

To bolster students' graduation rates, many colleges deploy safety nets for their students. Colleges know that sudden needs arise: A student's car breaks down, or they can't pay their rent for a month. As a result, many colleges have emergency aid available to help students get through these difficult, unexpected situations. Aid can come in the form of a grant or a no-interest loan. Colleges also may offer something called a completion or retention grant. These microgrants, which are typically under $2,000, are usually for students who do not have other aid or resources available and are one or two semesters away from graduation.

Colleges may also have financial policies for situations in which a student is unable to pay tuition or fees. At many colleges, the student's course schedule is cancelled, or a hold is placed on their account so they cannot register for any future courses. At some colleges, not paying a fee, regardless of the amount, results in a hold on the student's registration. In other words, if a student owes five dollars in a library fine, they cannot register for future courses.

These practices unfairly punish financially vulnerable students, for whom even a small fee or fine may be beyond their ability to pay. Colleges with a student-success orientation have mostly revised these policies to set a higher limit, such as $500, on what is owed to the college before academic registration is prevented. Moreover, colleges have established the option of payment plans, allowing the student to pay back the college in smaller pieces over a longer period. In addition, many colleges will disburse financial aid before or very early in the semester, understanding that late or delayed disbursement can derail a student's academic term.

Loans

Student loans are sums of money given to a student that need to be repaid, typically with interest. On average, roughly 70% of students graduate from college having taken out loans (Institute for College Access & Success, 2019). Most people get these loans through the federal government, though some get them from private banks. There are a few different types of federal loans. For some, particularly students from lower incomes, the government subsidizes the interest on the loan during college, which means the student doesn't pay interest on the loan until after graduation. The federal government also offers loans to parents, such as the Parent PLUS loan, to help pay for college costs for their students, though the interest rate on these loans is generally higher.

There are two key metrics regarding loans when evaluating a college: the average loan balance of college graduates and the loan default rate of the college. In other words, you'll want to know how much money students owe after they graduate and if they can pay back their loans after graduation. You can ask colleges for this information, and you can also get this information from the Department of Education's College Scorecard website.

Colleges with high levels of student success should have a loan default rate that is well below the national average. The excellent colleges have very low default rates, even for the students from the lowest income backgrounds. In some ways, these low rates indicate that the college was able to promote income and social mobility, helping students from lower incomes move to well-paid jobs where their salaries allow them to repay their loans.

HOW IS AID PRESENTED BY THE COLLEGE?

Colleges will often present prospective students with what is called an *aid package*, or a summary of all the aid they will be awarding to the student. These packages vary considerably based on the institution and student. As we have seen above, there are many types of aid. Two key measures of the college's package, of course, are how much the student and their family pays and what financial need would *not* be met if they accepted the aid package.

Depending on how these aid packages are calculated, they can be deceiving or present hurdles. For instance, a college may include loans as part of a student's financial aid package, even though loans have to be repaid. Or a college may offer a scholarship for the first year to get students to enroll at that college, but not continue the scholarship in subsequent years, leaving the student with a financial hole and at risk of leaving the college. A scholarship or other form of aid may have renewal criteria associated with it, such as a high GPA, that may put students at risk of losing their financial aid. (That said, some scholarship or grant aid renewal criteria, such as requiring a student to participate in experiential learning programs like the kind discussed in Chapter 5, may have positive impacts on student success.)

To get a sense of the actual amount students may pay to the college after aid, prospective students can also use what is known as a *net price calculator*. Virtually every college in the United States is required to display a calculator for students to determine their net price, or the price they will pay after subtracting scholarships and grants. The net price calculator is specific to each individual student; they input information to find out what their possible costs would be, unique to their circumstances. The U.S. Department of Education also maintains public data surrounding costs on their website, as well as the net price calculator for many colleges.

SHOULD YOU TAKE LOANS?

The commonness of student loan debt does not stop it from troubling many students, who worry that it may have a negative impact on their life after college. Indeed, the decision to take out loans during college requires thoughtful consideration.

Generally, U.S. federal government student loans can be helpful in promoting student success. While clearly not as beneficial as grants and scholarships, loans often provide the needed resources so students can fund their education, and because of this, research suggests they can boost academic performance and increase the likelihood of graduating (Marx & Turner, 2019).

Since loans may enable students to take more credit hours per semester, they can reduce the time it takes students to graduate. In addition, loans may enable a student to engage in an internship, research project, or other formative experience that both enriches their time in college and prepares them to launch successfully after graduation into a career or further education. In short, as Susan Dynarski writes in *The New York Times*, "Every college graduate would be better off without student debt. But they would not be better off without their college degrees, which loans make possible for millions of people" (2019, n.p.). At the same time, significant debt burden can have consequences across students' lives, impacting their likelihood of owning a home, the kinds of jobs they choose, when they are able to live independently, when they have children, and more (Min & Taylor, 2018).

To be sure, if a student takes a loan, it will need to be paid back with interest. But the interest rate on U.S. federal loans is modest compared to other loans. Moreover, the federal government offers income-based loan repayment plans, which means qualifying students will only need to repay loans at a rate that is proportional to their income. Federal loans can also have grace periods, stable interest rates, and forbearance options in case you lose a job. Private loans, meanwhile, typically do not offer these same protections and often have higher interest rates; they should be avoided unless absolutely necessary.

Since there are many high-quality public and private colleges that are either low cost or offer aid packages that substantially reduce a student's financial obligation, students should very carefully think through attending an institution where they will accumulate significant debt.

WORKING DURING COLLEGE

Many students with unmet financial need will not take loans, or will take limited loans, and often attempt to fund their education through work. Nationally, estimates are that about 70% of students in higher education, including both 2- and 4-year colleges, work during college at some point. Many of these students are from low-income and underrepresented backgrounds (Carnevale & Smith, 2018). Out of the undergraduates who work, 40% of them do so for at least 30 hours a week.

With the high cost of higher education, however, it is difficult for students to fund college from wages from work alone, or, as some people say, to work your way through college. While working during the summer may not interfere with students' academics, as they may not be actively taking classes, spending significant time during an academic semester working can get in the way of attending class, completing assignments, and engaging in experimental and formative learning opportunities. Many hours working in an off-campus position, particularly one that isn't connected to a student's educational or career objectives, can have a negative impact on student success (Carnevale & Smith, 2018). Only 45% of students who work more than 25 hours per week have a GPA above a B average. As students work more, the GPA tends to go down. The grades of low-income students can be especially affected by working significant hours. The Georgetown

Center on Education and the Workforce found that "59 percent of low-income students who work 15 hours or more . . . had a C average or lower" (Carnevale & Smith, 2018, p. 12).

Moreover, students who work more than 40 hours a week are half as likely to graduate compared to students who work less than 12 hours (Nova, 2019). Because students often take fewer credit hours per semester when holding time-intensive jobs, working more than 15 hours a week is associated with a longer time to graduation (Kyte, 2017).

To be clear, career exposure and meaningful work have an important role in a college education, providing context and application for classes, professional clarity for future goals, networking, and skills that help students thrive during and after college. Students need strong and well-articulated experiences on their resume and CV for employment and graduate school. And by working and building experiences during college, students may see some lift in their incomes after graduation (Douglas & Attewell, 2019).

Some colleges have enriched their student employment programs to make them more educational and career-building. For employment facilitated by the college, built-in reflection and regular guidance from a supervisor and others is incorporated. For instance, the University of Iowa's GROW (Guided Reflection on Work) program elevates the educational and career value of on-campus employment through structured and regular discussions between the student and the supervisor (Burnside et al., 2019).

If a student works, it is optimal for them to find part-time employment, paid internships, or remote work that aligns well with the skills and competencies that they need to develop for their educational and career goals. Of course, a student's personal circumstances may prevent them from being able to hold optimal jobs. This is compounded when resources from the college are insufficient to meet their financial needs. Some colleges have more sensitive aid packages and resources for students, such as on-campus childcare and employment opportunities, special grants or scholarships for students with dependents, and so on. If a student is in a situation to consider various colleges and has these kinds of needs, then evaluating the financial package and support a college offers is critical in deciding where to attend.

FACTORING IN GRADUATE SCHOOL

As students are making financial plans for college, they may also want to consider the future costs of graduate school. Because graduate school tuition is often more expensive than undergraduate studies, one paradigm is to stay at a lower-cost college for undergraduate and then pay a higher price for graduate school. While this might be a wise approach, the decision warrants thoughtful consideration.

It is important to remember that the undergraduate experience helps shape a student's aspirations and develops their academic, professional, and social skills. Sacrificing the quality of an undergraduate experience may have adverse effects. Imagine, for instance, you go to a college for your undergraduate degree that has weak and unsupportive practices toward student success. At these colleges, students run the risk of not developing their talents, not being competitive applicants for graduate school, or not graduating entirely. (As we discussed earlier in this chapter, there are many affordable colleges that prepare students for success upon graduation, so that paying a high amount isn't the only way to obtain a robust education.)

Moreover, it's not always the case that students need to pay significant amounts for graduate school. Just as with undergraduate programs, there are many lower-cost, high-quality graduate programs, and others with generous financial aid packages. In addition, it is common in the STEM majors for students to go from undergraduate directly to PhD programs. Colleges will typically waive tuition costs for PhD students and pay them a stipend as the student serves as a teaching or research assistant each semester.

Another complicating factor is that students' desires may change while they attend college. As a student progresses through their undergraduate career, they may find that their ambitions have shifted, such that they no longer desire the same graduate program they did when entering college—or graduate education at all. These kinds of shifts in students' academic interests are fairly common; data shows that about one-third of students change their major at least once in the first 3 years of college (National Center for Education Statistics, 2017b).

COLLEGES' RESOURCES FOR STUDENT FINANCIAL WELLNESS

For most students, making sure to spend money wisely is critical to their success. College is an investment, but it's easy and tempting to spend resources in ways that don't maximize your educational growth. Flush with an infusion of grant money in the beginning of a semester, a student may go out and buy all sorts of things and not be able to afford rent or books or something critical to their education.

Some students have little experience managing money or developing a budget before coming to college. As a result, colleges and other organizations have set up efforts to bolster students' financial literacy and wellness. A college oriented toward student success should have established efforts to help students with money management, creating budgets, and identifying financial priorities. One such example is the CashCourse program (www.cashcourse.org), developed by the National Endowment for Financial Education and available for free through many colleges. More advanced colleges have financial wellness and financial coaching programs that employ professionals or trained students who offer personalized consultations and planning.

As students have questions and need guidance, the college should have sufficient, trained financial counselors and advisors available to help students. A college that is marginal may have poorly managed offices, which result in long wait lines. At these institutions, there may not be proper protocol established to meet demand, or insufficient staff. Students will struggle to connect to resources, particularly during peak times, such as when aid is disbursed each term and there is an influx of student questions. These problems are warning signs that there are structural and staffing problems at the colleges, beyond just the arena of financial resources. An excellent college, by contrast, will have readily available staff. These colleges will also have enough data surfaced on their websites and through other resources that students are able to answer many questions themselves.

Overall, students and their families should look for colleges that are interested in supporting students financially all the way through to graduation. These are colleges that have financial aid and other offices that will work with students and provide aid, support, and guidance that is needed, including enough need-based aid to enable all students to fully engage in the college experience.

WHAT STUDENTS CAN DO BEFORE COLLEGE TO PREPARE

Before college, students can train and practice in money management, financial literacy, and financial wellness, setting reasonable expectations with their family and working to develop habits that will transfer into college. As students look to transition to college, they should set expectations for specific college expenses with their family. Students can also build savings and work experience that will help them engage more fully in the college experience.

THREE GUIDING QUESTIONS TO ASK ABOUT COSTS AND FINANCIAL AID

1. To what extent is the college and its activities affordable for you?
2. To what extent does the college have sufficient financial aid across the entire college experience to enable you to complete and engage fully in academic, personal, and professional opportunities?
3. To what extent does the college have resources and guidance available to help students cultivate financial literacy and wellness practices?

Table 8.1. A Rubric for Evaluating a College's Financial Support and Aid

Level	Indicators
Excellent	College transparently presents aid package and expectations across the full college experience; aid package is grant- and scholarship-based, rather than loan-based, and meets the full need of every student; college has robust funding for students' professional opportunities, as well as for students' emergencies; college has high-quality financial literacy and wellness training, including resources and guidance.
Good	College provides generous grant and scholarship aid such that few students are taking out loans; funding for students' professional opportunities and students' emergencies is largely available; the college provides quality financial management and wellness efforts for students.
Average	College offers a mix of merit- and need-based aid to students, but many students take loans and unmet need is still commonplace; funding for students' professional opportunities and students' emergencies is limited and not able to support many students; college has few financial literacy and wellness efforts.
Fair	College provides some aid to students, but there is still widespread unmet need; guidance and counseling to students is provided but insufficient, and there lacks any significant funding for students' professional opportunities or financial emergencies.
Poor	College offers very little financial aid for students, with minimal guidance in understanding costs, applying for and managing federal or state aid, or building financial literacy and wellness; significant unmet need among the student body impairs student success.

CHAPTER 9

Success After College

Employment, Further Education, and Beyond

Jane spent her 4 years at college learning and having fun. When she wasn't in class, she was spending time with her friends or playing intramural sports. She was a good student, but not particularly academically involved. A few weeks before graduation, she tuned into her classmates' conversation about plans after graduation. It turned out they had been applying to internships, going to career fairs, and interviewing at different companies throughout the semester. Jane had no idea she was supposed to be doing any of that. She asked to meet with an advisor just 2 weeks before graduation. Her question seemed simple: "I'm about to graduate; what do I do now?"

Many colleges have not embraced their role in affecting the launch of students after graduation into employment or further education. These colleges may say they were successful if they get a student to graduation, with little consideration of dimensions of student development. But as we've discussed with other areas of the college experience, absent an intentional, effective approach to student success, colleges will end up leaving students behind. Students, particularly ones from lower-income or first-generation backgrounds, may have little idea of how to go about building a competitive resume, developing sought-after skills, engaging in formative experiences, and communicating their skills in ways that are compelling. Without proper guidance, students can end up floundering as they graduate, lacking direction or clarity about what to do next.

Thus far, we've focused on success during college. Now we turn to success after college: What dimensions of the college experience impact students' postgraduation outcomes, and what should colleges be doing to elevate the outcomes of students after they graduate?

HOW TO APPROACH AND EVALUATE COLLEGES' CAREER SERVICES

Many colleges invest considerably into providing career and professional support for their students. Below, we'll break down some of the key components of career services in higher education to look for when examining colleges.

Career counseling for college students as a field has developed into a sophisticated practice. After all, helping a young person discern a vocation and align their life toward that end can often be entangled with a host of familial, social, personal, and other complexities. A skilled professional, such as those at many college career centers, should have the time and experience to help students disentangle their goals from external pressures and envision a path forward. In other words, career centers should help students articulate how they envision success and develop a game plan to actualize it.

Many students may not know the norms of seeking a job, the range of potential career fields and subfields, models of different careers, or what their salary expectations should be. In offering guidance, colleges can help build and facilitate experiences for their students. Part of this guidance should include connecting students to experiential learning opportunities and activities, as discussed in Chapters 5 and 6, which can increase career outcomes (Miller et al., 2017). A college should have sufficient trained professional staff to meet students' complex needs.

Beyond career counseling, there are many other services that career center staff can provide. They can help connect students with career opportunities and help them tailor application materials. This can include developing an academic curriculum vitae, which is typically used when applying to graduate schools; editing resumes and cover letters; or bringing employers directly onto campuses. Excellent colleges offer robust and tailored career fairs or recruiting events, which may occur on-campus or remotely. Participating students get a sense of what kinds of opportunities exist and begin building relationships with employers.

At the University of Connecticut, for example, there are general career fairs in the fall and spring. The college also offers more specialized fairs. A student interested in a career in marine biology can attend the STEM career fair, while someone interested in working with youth experiencing homelessness can go to the Non-Profit and Service Fair (University of Connecticut, n.d.). As you think about different colleges, consider whether they have relationships with a wide range of employers across different industries and how they use these connections to help students.

Mock interviews help students prepare for the process of interviewing for positions. The structure of interviews, the types of questions asked, and what an employer hopes to see in a candidate may be unfamiliar to students. Mock interviews can help students feel more at ease in these environments because they have practiced answering common questions and received feedback on their performances. Colleges can also provide students professional clothing to use because buying professional clothing can be a barrier. Some simply don't have the disposable income to purchase new suits or dresses, while others come from backgrounds where a business professional dress code is unfamiliar. Fresno State in California, for instance, operates its Clothing Closet, which provides students with the proper attire for interviews and first jobs. Staff there can guide students toward appropriate options for their professional opportunities. Students at Fresno State can take three articles of clothing for free each semester, while others can donate their own gently used clothes or make cash donations (Fresno State, n.d.).

When colleges foster opportunities for students to engage in networking, students connect with potential employers and alumni, while learning how to build professional relationships. Substantive engagement with alumni and professionals can take a variety of forms. Many colleges have formal alumni associations or other networks or groups for alumni of their college. Since these networks can open opportunities for students, prospective students should consider a college's alumni and professional networks and the extent to which they are active, engaged, connected, and effective in supporting students in reaching their goals. Students, for example, can meet professionals through panels, programming, and events, but also through college-organized trips to visit companies. Some colleges take students to New York City to meet with leading companies in the financial industry. Colleges also may facilitate informational interviews with industry professionals to learn more about a field, company, or position in a less formal setting. These opportunities give students ways to connect with people in fields they may be interested in pursuing, or in fields they may have never known existed. For instance, Florida State University held a "Doctor's Corner" event for students who are the first ones in their families to attend college. While many students are familiar with doctors who have MD degrees, they may not know that other kinds of doctorates exist. The event had students hear from, engage, and have dinner with alumni who have doctorates of various kinds in healthcare, such as the Doctor of Medicine degree (MD) and Doctor of Physical Therapy degree (DPT), but also a Doctor of Education degree (EdD), a Doctor of Philosophy degree (PhD), a Juris Doctor degree (JD), and more.

These sorts of programming should help students understand the difference between engaging in superficial "networking" and actually building a network. Some students think that shaking a lot of hands at an event or collecting dozens of business cards is substantial networking when, in reality, this may do little to help them forge meaningful connections. Instead, students should strive to develop impactful relationships with people in college and beyond, particularly with those who will advocate for them and connect them to opportunities for their advancement.

But professional career advising staff alone may not be enough to meet the diverse needs of students—and some students may not require a high level of specialized assistance. A number of people at the college can add valuable perspectives. These include, among others, professors, alumni, and mentors from the professional community. A college can empower its faculty members to have conversations about career development with students, including graduate education. A college can also have robust alumni and other mentors from various industries who can be available to give students guidance on campus or remotely. Students and their families can ask colleges directly to explain the various ways they facilitate alumni engagement with students and how that engagement advances student success.

Colleges should also help students consider, prepare for, and enter graduate school and further education. This is particularly true for industries in which having a master's degree is expected. Colleges should support students preparing for the needed exams, perhaps providing free or highly subsidized test preparation for students. Colleges may offer pathway programs that enable students to build graduate education into their bachelor's program, such as 3+1 or 4+1 pathways that allow a student to earn a bachelor's and master's degree in 4 or 5 years, as discussed in Chapter 3.

While it may be tempting for students to wait until their senior year of college to engage in career-building activities, such as mentoring, career counseling, and alumni engagement, it is important to start this early in college and to continue throughout. Feeling at home in a career pathway can increase students' motivation and sense of belonging in college. Research from education best practice firm EAB has also found that the earlier a student starts searching for employment, the better (Bowen, 2019). They found that students who began searching for a job 1 year prior to graduation had a 15% higher chance of positive employment outcomes, compared to those who started searching later. Students who sought out opportunities early were also more likely to have a full-time, higher-paying job that required a college degree, and have more job satisfaction.

Still, there may be intensive and unique needs that arise as the student approaches and enters the job or graduate school search, application, and acceptance process. Student success–oriented colleges recognize this and provide special resources to students in their final year. For instance, Tulane University has professional staff as part of their Senior Year Experience program who provide structured, intensive guidance. Staff meet regularly with students during their last year as they navigate the career process and launch from the college. They empower their students to set goals and stay accountable to achieving them, overcoming obstacles and finding solutions.

MATCHING QUALIFICATIONS TO POSTGRADUATION OUTCOMES

Without the right guidance, mentorship, and preparation, students will often end up in jobs or graduate schools that don't match their levels of qualification. This happens, for instance, when a highly talented student ends up in an entry-level role that doesn't require a bachelor's degree, when they could have had a job that was higher paying with more upward mobility and aligned with their talents. Research suggests that these outcomes, what some call "underemployment," can actually be quite common, with up to 43% of college graduates in roles that don't require a bachelor's degree in their first job after college. Unfortunately, starting off in these sorts of roles can have long-term impacts for salaries and mobility, with many of these students persisting in jobs that don't require a bachelor's degree even 5 or 10 years later (Sigelman et al., 2018).

Take Sam and Daniel, a pair of twins who attended different colleges. Sam attended a college that had average support for its students. At the beginning of Sam's collegiate career, he was not certain of what he wanted to do after graduation, and he rarely received much guidance. However, in his senior year, Sam began to seriously think about life after graduation, and he visited the career services office in his college. He met with an advisor, who helped him assess his academic and extracurricular achievements. With help from the office, Sam put together a resume, highlighting a student club he was in, the key courses he took, and projects he worked on, as well as the service-industry job he held during college. He figured that a college degree would be enough, and he applied broadly across a number of industries and companies to find a job after graduation, but he struggled to get a role, as hiring managers were screening for particular experiences and keywords. Eventually, he secured an entry-level service role at a company, happy to have found something.

Meanwhile, Daniel attended a college that has highly mature support for students' postgraduation planning and development. Daniel received early and deep mentorship, starting in his first year. During meetings with his favorite professor, he had regular discussions about life after college, employment opportunities, and the skills he wanted to develop, as well as the impact he wanted to make in the world and how his skills aligned with it. Daniel worked with his advisors, and he got advice from college alumni and other professionals to plan out the kind of courses, internships, international study, community service, and research experiences he should undertake to develop those skills along the way. The college provided funding for Daniel to have these experiences. When he did an unpaid internship in Congress one summer, the college even adjusted for lost income he would have received.

During his sophomore year, Daniel became interested in a management consulting career after college. The college connected him with key alumni in that role, and he learned that his top company, McKinsey & Company, had an earlier recruitment cycle than most companies. The college worked with Daniel to craft a tailored resume, highlighting the diverse range of career-building and professional experiences and the core, demonstrable outcomes from each experience. The college also helped him build a robust portfolio to showcase examples of his work.

Finally, Daniel met with a recruiter from the company when he attended an on-campus career recruitment event and landed an interview. The college arranged practice interviews, including with an alumnus who helped him prepare for the unique interview, which required on-the-spot problem solving and analysis. Daniel was excited to start the position and grateful for all the guidance and support from his college along the way.

WHAT DO EMPLOYERS LOOK FOR IN STUDENTS?

In response to the demands for colleges to prepare students for employment, colleges and employers have come together to inventory the skills that colleges should be developing in students. The National Association of Colleges and Employers (NACE) developed a set of common competencies of what employers are seeking in students in one such effort (NACE, n.d.). The NACE team's list includes both technical and non-technical skills that help students "future-proof" themselves and develop cross-cutting skills that allow for growth and career mobility over time, as circumstances change and technology evolves.

These competencies are teamwork and collaboration; oral and written communication; work ethic and professionalism; and critical thinking and problem solving, as well as proficiency with digital technology and leadership. Another competency is career management, which is the ability to navigate career opportunities and seek professional growth. A person who has this competency would be able to clearly articulate their professional strengths and weaknesses in an interview, for instance. The last competency is global and intercultural fluency, which emphasizes how people can be empowered to work effectively and empathetically across cultures and with diverse groups of people.

During college, these competencies can be integrated into the curricular and co-curricular experience. Colleges can intentionally foster the development of these competencies through assignments, courses, and internships. In some programs, often those designed for first-year students, students are asked to develop and reflect on specific plans to develop these competencies over their undergraduate career.

Employers want students to be able to articulate their skills; colleges can help students do this through fostering regular reflection and showcasing projects they produce. E-portfolios and career portfolios allow students to digitally collect their work throughout college, reflect on their growth from that work, and highlight pieces with selected audiences, such as employers or advisors. Students can also use these e-portfolios to feature learning from extracurriculars and activities outside of the classroom, connecting their development to experiences across different settings. This kind of regular reflection enables students to articulate more fully their experiences and how they align with an employment or graduate school opportunity. When a potential employer asks a student, "What did you learn from your internship?" the student will have already practiced speaking about how experiential learning furthered their development and gave them transferable skills for the job market.

There are several ways students can showcase skill development for employers or selection committees outside of gaining a designation on their transcript. Colleges, for instance, can award digital badges, or virtual recognition of a certain skill that a student developed, such as proficiency with 3D printing.

CIVIC DEVELOPMENT: MAKING CONTRIBUTIONS AFTER COLLEGE

The fundamental skills that one needs in their career overlap with the skills one needs in civic and community life. Students, employees, and indeed everyone needs to be able to express their thoughts, work with diverse others, problem-solve, and more. College can develop the fundamental skills that prepare people for both work and civic participation, reminding students of their potential and improving their ability to contribute positively to the lives of others.

Students can also make civic development a part of their everyday experience in college, as they live with others and practice their ability to deeply understand them. Students can aim to take courses, engage in community service, and participate in educational experiences that help them develop their sense of self within a larger community and global context.

THREE GUIDING QUESTIONS TO ASK ABOUT EMPLOYMENT, FURTHER EDUCATION, AND BEYOND

1. To what extent does the college have strong postgraduation outcomes for its students?
2. To what extent does the college cultivate students' competencies and skills for long-term career and life success?
3. To what extent does the college have sufficient personnel and programming to help students engage in career-building activities and successfully navigate their launch from college?

Table 9.1. A Rubric for Evaluating a College's Postgraduation Success Efforts

Level	Indicators
Excellent	College has clearly articulated skill development aligned with high-quality programming in and outside of courses that cultivate students' career and civic competencies; strong, proactive, and personalized advising and mentoring exists to prepare students for postgraduation life; services are sufficient to meet the diverse needs of the student body; opportunities to build connections with a wide range of employers and professionals are widespread.
Good	College has widely deployed practices that prepare students for postgraduation life; there are pockets of excellence in programming and advising, but gaps exist in supporting the diverse needs of the student body; college often offers opportunities for students to build connections with a wide range of employers and professionals.
Average	College has a focus on skill development for postgraduation success, but it lacks sufficient staff to fully deploy quality programming or advising efforts across the student body or to support the range of students' postgraduation goals; there are professional networking and career development opportunities available, but their limited capacity restricts student participation.
Fair	College acknowledges its role in preparing students for postgraduation life; the limited availability of services and programming significantly restricts student participation and curtails student development skills and competencies for postgraduation success.
Poor	College takes limited responsibility to help prepare students for life after graduation and has little explicit activity designed to bolster the postgraduation outcomes of students.

Concluding Thoughts

When college doesn't go right, people are quick to blame the student. But we've learned that colleges themselves have a major role in student success too. They can be organized and run in such a way that they can derail a student. And many colleges do just that: They don't even get the basic stuff right, like offering enough courses to enable on-time graduation, much less provide the life-changing instruction and experiential learning crucial to student growth. In short, too many colleges admit students but treat them poorly, failing to deliver on the promise of higher education.

Fortunately, many colleges have reformed themselves, launched new initiatives, redesigned student experiences, and developed comprehensive strategies to elevate student growth and development. These efforts take many forms, but as we have reviewed in this book, they must be thoughtful, coherent, and coordinated, building on one another to promote students' full development and reinforced by a culture where *every student matters*. With the right balance of engagement, challenge, and support, colleges can promote the success of all students.

So how do you do college right? By choosing a college that is designed for your success, and by prioritizing and engaging in the experiences that promote it.

With this book, you have the framework to evaluate what's important. You can push colleges to be better by asking deeper questions and by expecting more from your higher education institutions. Students can choose a college where they can grow to their full potential, and they can be deliberate and purposeful about how they spend their time there. Students can leave higher education with the mentors, skills, and dispositions to thrive after college and help address the major challenges we are facing in the world. But college isn't all about maximizing potential—students can have fun along the way, building lifelong friendships and engaging in novel activities.

Together, we can set new and high expectations for colleges and elevate the quality of the student experience. Now get out there—a great college education is waiting to be crafted!

Brief Glossary of Student Success Terms

Active Learning: In contrast to traditional, passive lecturing, active learning refers to teaching that engages the students during class. Active learning is participatory and encourages students to interact with each other and course materials.

Advising: A process in which a trained professional or peer helps a student ensure completion of their degree, maximize their time in higher education, or prepare for life after college. Elements of advising include guidance on selecting courses and how to access a college's resources, such as financial aid or counseling.

Career Services: Programming and assistance to help students develop, prepare for, and secure their further educational and career goals.

Competencies: The skills a student develops as a result of an educational activity that enable them to undertake future personal and professional endeavors. Examples include oral and written communication, critical thinking, teamwork, and problem solving.

Cost of Attendance: The estimated annual cost of attending a particular college, including expenses related to tuition, housing, transportation, textbooks, and more.

Curriculum: The set of academic courses students take at a college. Curriculums vary based on the requirements of a student's major or degree.

Disparities: Refers to the rates in which different student groups achieve success at a college. Disparities may be seen at several levels, such as participation in certain programs, gaps in course completion rates, and differences in graduation rates.

Every-Student-Matters Culture: Refers to a college culture in which all students are cared about and their success is a top priority.

The success of every student is seen as integral to the overall success of the college.

Expected Family Contribution (EFC): The amount of money the U.S. federal government expects a student or student's family to pay toward the cost of their college education. The figure is used in calculating financial aid eligibility.

Experiential Learning: A form of learning that takes place outside of the traditional classroom setting, including internships, study abroad, undergraduate research, service-learning, and other professional and creative work experiences.

Fellowship: Refers to competitive scholarships and awards, such as the Rhodes, Fulbright, and Truman Scholarships. Often these awards help pay for college or graduate school and bring recipients together for special programming.

Financial Aid Package: The total amount of financial aid a student is offered, including scholarships, tuition waivers, grants, loans, and work-study opportunities.

First-Generation Student: A student whose parent(s) or guardian(s) have not earned a college degree.

Free Application for Federal Student Aid (FAFSA): A U.S. federal government form students complete to determine their eligibility for student financial aid.

General Education: Refers to the broad set of courses, generally taken during the first 2 years, that the college considers to be foundational to education and to prepare students for life. General education requirements typically include courses with a focus on history, diversity, writing, math, sciences, and more.

Graduation Rate: Refers to the percentage of students who complete their degree at a college, typically presented in how many students complete their degrees in 4 or 6 years.

Grants: Sums of money that are typically awarded to students with financial need. Grants do not need to be repaid.

Growth Mindset: The belief that one can get better at tasks or subjects through practice and learning from errors.

Guided Pathway: An articulated semester-by-semester set of courses in the curriculum that a student should sequentially move through within their major in order to graduate. It may also be referred to as an academic map or major map.

High-Impact Practices (HIPs): Educational activities in colleges that research has identified as promoting deep learning and improved student outcomes during and after college, such as experiential learning, capstone courses, and collaborative projects.

Internship: A learning experience with an organization in a professional setting, providing students valuable work experiences. Internships can also help students make connections in professional fields and clarify educational or career goals.

Learning Community: Refers to structured programming that aims to bring together relatively small groups of students with common interests, majors, or activities. Learning communities are commonly offered for first-year students and include courses participants take together.

Learning Outcomes: Statements that describe the skills and knowledge students are expected to demonstrate as the result of successfully completing a course or other educational activity.

Life Coach: A trained professional who meets with students on a regular basis to help them identify and reach their goals. Life coaches, also known as success coaches, challenge and support students while helping them develop an individualized success plan, while providing support and accountability.

Loan: Sum of money provided to a student that needs to be repaid, typically with interest.

Major: A set of courses that a student takes to earn a degree in a certain field of study. In order to complete a major, students must complete required and elective courses established by the college. Some majors may have restricted enrollment and thus a competitive admissions process.

Net Price: The price a student is expected to pay for college after deducting any scholarships, grants, or waivers the student is receiving.

Office Hours: Times outside of class at which the course instructor is scheduled to be available to engage with, offer guidance to, and answer questions from students. Typically, office hours are held in the instructor's office, but they can also be offered online or at other locations.

Orientation: Educational programming at the start of a student's college journey to help them successfully transition to the college.

Programming often includes learning about the college and available resources, connecting with peers, and ensuring academic course registration.

Postgraduation Outcomes: Refers to what students do after graduation from college. Commonly, the employment and further educational achievements of students are measured.

Prerequisite Courses: Academic courses that must be completed prior to enrolling in a particular subsequent course, set of courses, or major.

Ranking: A college's position on a list that assesses colleges according to certain criteria, such as graduation rates and student-to-faculty ratios.

Retention Rate: The percentage of a college's first-year students who continue to their second year.

Scholarships: Monetary awards given to students to help them pay for college expenses, generally given by colleges, governments, or other outside organizations.

Sense of Belonging: Refers to a student's feeling that they matter to a college and that they are connected to their peers, faculty, and institution.

Service Learning: A teaching approach in which a course integrates community service with instruction and guided student reflection. Service learning gives students direct experience with issues they are studying and empowers them to understand the complex challenges communities face.

Student Success: Includes the full development of students across professional, intellectual, civic, and personal domains. Success is often measured by the rate at which students graduate and achieve meaningful outcomes after graduation.

Study Abroad: Refers to educational activities that take place outside of the colleges' home country and are completed as part of students' degree program. While most study abroad programs take the form of classroom study, there are also research, internship, and service-learning programs.

Tutoring: Occurs when a peer, faculty member, or professional provides tailored academic assistance to one or more students on a specific subject.

Undergraduate Research: When an undergraduate student conducts a research or creative project under the mentorship of a professor or other researcher. Students may undertake their own original research projects or assist researchers with their existing work.

Underrepresented Students: Students who are not proportionally enrolled in higher education or historically did not have access to a college education. Underrepresented student groups generally include those who are the first in their families to attend college or those who are part of ethnic or racial minority groups.

Wellness: A holistic understanding of the students' mental, physical, emotional, and overall well-being and health.

Work-Study Programs: College-run programs, funded with federal, state, or college money, in which students work on- or off-campus part-time to help pay for college expenses.

References

Abel, J. R., & Deitz, R. (2014, September 03). Staying in college longer than four years costs more than you might think [Blog post]. *Liberty Street Economics.* Federal Reserve Bank of New York. libertystreeteconomics. newyorkfed.org/2014/09/staying-in-college-longer-than-four-years-costs-more-than-you-might-think.html

Abel, J. R., & Deitz, R. (2016). *Underemployment in the early careers of college graduates following the great recession.* (NBER Working Paper No. 22654). National Bureau of Economic Research. www.nber.org/papers/w22654

Agnes Scott College. (2015). *Leading in a global society: Agnes Scott reinvents the liberal arts for the 21st century.* www.agnesscott.edu/about/strategicplan/ files/documents/Strategic%20Plan%20FINAL%2010-30-15%20 with%20logo1.pdf

Ambrose, S., Bridges, M., Lovett, M., DiPietro, M., & Norman, M. (2010). *How learning works: Seven research-based principles for smart teaching.* Jossey-Bass.

American College Health Association. (2018). *Spring 2018 reference group executive summary.* www.acha.org/documents/ncha/NCHA-II_Spring_2018_ Reference_Group_Executive_Summary.pdf

American Psychological Association. (2020, February 01). Building your resilience. www.apa.org/topics/resilience

Arnett, J. J. (2004). *Emerging adulthood: The winding road from the late teens through the twenties.* Oxford University Press.

Astin, A. W. (1977). *Four critical years: Effects of college on beliefs, attitudes, and knowledge.* John Wiley & Sons.

Bahls, S. C. (2019, July). Demystifying rankings and ratings. *Trusteeship, 27*(4), 30–36. agb.org/trusteeship-article/demystifying-rankings-and-ratings/

Bailey, T. R., Jaggars, S. S., & Jenkins, D. (2015). *Redesigning America's community colleges: A clearer path to student success.* Harvard University Press.

Barefoot, B. O., & Fidler, P. P. (1992). *National Survey of Freshman Seminar Programming, 1991. Helping First Year College Students Climb the Academic Ladder.* The Freshman Year Experience: Monograph Series Number 10. National Resource Center for the Freshman Year Experience. eric.ed.gov /?id=ED354842

Baumeister, R. F., & Leary, M. R. (1995). The need to belong: Desire for interpersonal attachments as a fundamental human motivation. *Psychological Bulletin, 117*(3), 497–529. doi.org/10.1037/0033-2909.117.3.497

Becker, M. S. (2020, January 06). The mental health crisis on campus and how colleges can fix it. *The Conversation.* theconversation.com/the-mental-health-crisis-on-campus-and-how-colleges-can-fix-it-127875

Benton, S. L., & Pallett, W. H. (2013, January 29). Class size matters. *Inside Higher Ed.* www.insidehighered.com/views/2013/01/29/essay-importance-class-size-higher-education

Bethune, S. (2019, January). Gen Z more likely to report mental health concerns. *Monitor on Psychology, 50*(1), 20. www.apa.org/monitor/2019/01/gen-z

Birditt, K. S., Fingerman, K. L., Lefkowitz, E. S., & Dush, C. M. (2008). Parents perceived as peers: Filial maturity in adulthood. *Journal of Adult Development, 15*(1), 1–12. doi.org/10.1007/s10804-007-9019-2

Boisjoly, J., Duncan, G. J., Kremer, M., Levy, D. M., & Eccles, J. (2006). Empathy or antipathy? The impact of diversity. *American Economic Review, 96*(5), 1890–1905. doi.org/10.1257/aer.96.5.1890

Bowen, M. (2019, November 18). These three activities could help improve post-graduate outcomes [Blog post]. EAB. eab.com/insights/blogs/student-success/these-three-activities-could-help-improve-post-graduate-outcomes/

Bowie, L. (2018, Feb 28). UMBC's Freeman Hrabowski receives national lifetime achievement award. *Baltimore Sun.* https://www.baltimoresun.com/education/bs-md-co-freeman-hrabowski-award-20180227-story.html

Bradley-Geist, J. C., & Olson-Buchanan, J. B. (2014). Helicopter parents: An examination of the correlates of over-parenting of college students. *Education Training, 56*(4), 314–328. doi.org/10.1108/et-10-2012-0096

Brooks, K. (2012, August 05). Why major in history? *Psychology Today.* https://www.psychologytoday.com/us/blog/career-transitions/201208/why-major-in-history

Brown, S. (2020, January 14). Students are showing up at counseling centers in droves. But they don't always get the treatment they need. *Chronicle of Higher Education.* www.chronicle.com/article/Students-Are-Showing-Up-at/247844

Brownson, C., Drum, D. J., Becker, M. A., Saathoff, A., & Hentschel, E. (2016). Distress and suicidality in higher education: Implications for population-oriented prevention paradigms. *Journal of College Student Psychotherapy, 30*(2), 98–113. doi.org/10.1080/87568225.2016.1140978

Bughin, J., Hazan, E., Lund, S., Dahlström, P., Wiesinger, A., & Subramaniam, A. (2018). *Skill shift: Automation and the future of the workforce.* McKinsey & Company. www.mckinsey.com/featured-insights/future-of-work/skill-shift-automation-and-the-future-of-the-workforce

Burnside, O., Wesley, A., Wesaw, A., & Parnell, A. (2019). *Employing student success: A comprehensive examination of on-campus student employment.* NASPA.

www.naspa.org/report/employing-student-success-a-comprehensive-examination-of-on-campus-student-employment

Busteed, B. (2019, February 25). Dear faculty: You matter more than you know. *Inside Higher Ed.* www.insidehighered.com/views/2019/02/25/faculty-mentors-provide-students-exceptional-educational-benefits-opinion

Canaan, S., Deeb, A., & Mouganie, P. (2019). Advisor value-added and student outcomes: Evidence from randomly assigned college advisors. *SSRN Electronic Journal.* doi.org/10.2139/ssrn.3478331

Canning, E. A., Muenks, K., Green, D. J., & Murphy, M. C. (2019). STEM faculty who believe ability is fixed have larger racial achievement gaps and inspire less student motivation in their classes. *Science Advances, 5*(2). doi.org/10.1126/sciadv.aau4734

Carnevale, A. P., Cheah, B., & Hanson, A. (2015). *The economic value of college majors.* Georgetown University Center on Education and the Workforce. cew.georgetown.edu/cew-reports/valueofcollegemajors

Carnevale, A. P., & Smith, N. (2018). *Balancing work and learning: Implications for low-income students.* Georgetown University Center on Education and the Workforce. cew.georgetown.edu/cew-reports/learnandearn

Center for the Advancement of Teaching. (2019a, September 13). Checking in. teaching.fsu.edu/tips/2019/09/13/checking-in

Center for the Advancement of Teaching. (2019b, October 04). You're the thermostat. teaching.fsu.edu/tips/2019/10/04/youre-the-thermostat/

Challenge Success. (2018). *A "fit" over rankings: Why college engagement matters more than selectivity.* ed.stanford.edu/sites/default/files/challenge_success_white_paper_on_college_admissions_10.1.2018-reduced.pdf

Chicago Tribune Staff. (2019, April 03). Does where you go to college really matter? We asked 10 Chicago CEOs. *Chicago Tribune.* https://www.chicagotribune.com/business/ct-biz-ceos-illinois-where-went-to-college-20190327-story.html

Chickering, A.W., & Gamson, Z.F. (1987). Seven principles for good practice in undergraduate education. *AAHE Bulletin, 39*(7), 3–7.

Chickering, A. W., & Gamson, Z. F. (1991). Applying the seven principles for good practice in undergraduate education. *New Directions in Teaching & Learning,* 47.

Coffey, C., Sentz, R., & Saleh, Y. (2019, August 01). *Degrees at work: Examining the serendipitous outcomes of diverse degrees.* Emsi. www.economicmodeling.com/wp-content/uploads/2019/08/Emsi_Degrees-at-Work_Full-Report-1.pdf

College Board. (2019). *Trends in college pricing 2019.* research.collegeboard.org/pdf/trends-college-pricing-2019-full-report.pdf

College Pulse. (2019, May 12). 7 charts to explain college students' relationships with their mothers. https://wordpress.collegepulse.com/2019/05/7-statistics-for-mothers-on-mothers-day.html

College Support Program (n.d.) About CSP. gsapp.rutgers.edu/centers-clinical-services/college-support-program/about-csp

Council on Undergraduate Research. (n.d.). Mission. www.cur.org/who/organization/mission/

Dedman, B. (2019, February 06). The impacts of project-based learning at Worcester Polytechnic Institute. *AAC&U Newsletter*. www.aacu.org/aacu-news/newsletter/2019/february/campus-model

Deming, D., & Noray, K. (2019). STEM careers and the changing skill requirements of work. HKS Working Paper No. RWP19-025. doi.org/10.2139/ssrn.3451346

Denning, J. T., Marx, B. M., & Turner, L. J. (2019). Propelled: The effects of grants on graduation, earnings, and welfare. *American Economic Journal: Applied Economics, 11*(3), 193–224. doi.org/10.1257/app.20180100

DePaul University. (n.d.). Combined Bachelor's and Master's in Marketing. business.depaul.edu/academics/marketing/combined-degree-program/Pages/combined-marketing-degree.aspx

Derryberry, W. P., & Thoma, S. J. (2000). The friendship effect: Its role in the development of moral thinking in students. *About Campus, 5*(2), 13–18. doi.org/10.1177/108648220000500204

Deslauriers, L., McCarty, L. S., Miller, K., Callaghan, K., & Kestin, G. (2019). Measuring actual learning versus feeling of learning in response to being actively engaged in the classroom. *Proceedings of the National Academy of Sciences, 116*(39), 19251–19257. doi.org/10.1073/pnas.1821936116

Douglas, D., & Attewell, P. (2019). The relationship between work during college and post college earnings. *Frontiers in Sociology, 4*. doi.org/10.3389/fsoc.2019.00078

Downs, N., Galles, E., Skehan, B., & Lipson, S. K. (2018). Be true to our schools—models of care in college mental health. *Current Psychiatry Reports, 20*(9). doi.org/10.1007/s11920-018-0935-6

Dwyer, M. (2004). More is better: The impact of study abroad duration. *Frontiers: The Interdisciplinary Journal of Study Abroad, 10*, 151–163. eric.ed.gov/?id=EJ891454

Dynarski, S. (2019, September 6). Taking out a student loan is better than dropping out. *The New York Times*. www.nytimes.com/2019/09/06/business/student-loans-needed-community-colleges.html

EAB. (2019, December 5). *Build resilience, reduce early attrition in less than an hour*. eab.com/insights/daily-briefing/student-success/build-resilience-reduce-early-attrition-in-less-than-an-hour/

Eagan, K., Stolzenberg, E. B., Ramirez, J. J., Aragon, M. C., Suchard, M. R., & Hurtado, S. (2014). *The American freshman: National norms fall 2014*. Higher Education Research Institute, UCLA. www.heri.ucla.edu/monographs/TheAmericanFreshman2014.pdf

Elfman, L. (2019, October 10). Study Finds College Students Build Friendships that Bridge Divides. Diverse Education. https://diverseeducation.com/article/156973/

Escarcha, K. (2019, November 19). *3 things students experiencing homelessness need campus leaders to know*. EAB. eab.com/insights/daily-briefing/student-success/support-students-experiencing-homelessness/

Even, W. E., & Smith, A. (2018). Greek life, academics, and earnings. *SSRN Electronic Journal*. doi.org/10.2139/ssrn.3257025

Excelencia in Education (n.d.). *Growing what works database*. www.edexcelencia.org/programs-initiatives/growing-what-works-database

Finley, A. P., & McNair, T. (2013). *Assessing underserved students' engagement in high-impact practices*. Association of American Colleges and Universities. www.aacu.org/sites/default/files/files/assessinghips/AssessingHIPS_TG-GrantReport.pdf

Fischer, M. (2017, April 7). *How one university promoted student retention with community-centric residence halls*. EAB. eab.com/insights/expert-insight/facilities/how-one-university-promoted-student-retention-with-community-centric-residence-halls/

Fish, S. E. (2012). *Save the world on your own time*. Oxford University Press.

Florida State University (n.d.). *Recognized student organizations*. https://union.fsu.edu/sac/involvement

Florida State University Registrar (2019). *2019–2020 general bulletin, undergraduate edition*. registrar.fsu.edu/archive/bulletin/undergraduate/2019_gen_bulletin.pdf

Freeman, S., Eddy, S. L., McDonough, M., Smith, M. K., Okoroafor, N., Jordt, H., & Wenderoth, M. P. (2014). Active learning increases student performance in science, engineering, and mathematics. *Proceedings of the National Academy of Sciences, 111*(23), 8410–8415. doi.org/10.1073/pnas.1319030111

Freishtat, R. (2020, January 14). *Don't be alone during office hours*. Berkeley Center for Teaching and Learning. https://teaching.berkeley.edu/news/dont-be-alone-during-office-hours-0

Fresno State. (n.d.). *Clothing closet*. http://www.fresnostate.edu/studentaffairs/careers/closet.html

Gap Year Association. (n.d.). *Accredited gap year programs*. www.gapyearassociation.org/gap-year-programs.php

George Mason University. (2017, December). *2014-2024 strategic plan: 2017 update*. https://strategicplan.gmu.edu/wp-content/uploads/2017/12/Strategic-Plan-Update-BOV-Final.pdf

Goldrick-Rab, S., Baker-Smith, C., Coca, V., Looker, E., & Williams, T. (2019, April 30). *College and university basic needs insecurity: A national #RealCollege survey report*. The Hope Center for College, Community, and Justice. hope4college.com/college-and-university-basic-needs-insecurity-a-national-realcollege-survey-report/

Gopalan, M., & Brady, S. T. (2019). College students' sense of belonging: A national perspective. *Educational Researcher, 49*(2). doi.org/10.3102/0013189x19897622

Guidubaldi, J. (2020). Garnet and Gold Scholars Society Synthesis Reflection. Florida State University. Unpublished.

Hagedorn, L. S., Chi, W. Y., Cepeda, R. M., & McLain, M. (2007). An investigation of critical mass: The role of Latino representation in the success of urban community college students. *Research in Higher Education, 48*(1), 73–91. doi.org/10.1007/s11162-006-9024-5

Harnisch, T. L., & Lebioda, K. (2016). *Top 10 higher education state policy issues for 2016. Higher education policy brief.* American Association of State Colleges and Universities. luminafoundation.org/wp-content/uploads/2017/08/top10-higher-ed-state-policy-issues-2016.pdf

Heath, M. (2018, October 10). FAFSA completion in Utah increases for second year in a row. Utah System of Higher Education. ushe.edu/fafsa-completion-in-utah-inceases-second-year/

Hurtado, S. (2001). Linking diversity and educational purpose: How diversity affects the classroom environment and student development. In G. Orfield (Ed.), *Diversity challenged: Evidence on the impact of affirmative action* (pp. 187–204). Civil Rights Project, Harvard University. files.eric.ed.gov/fulltext/ED456199.pdf

Institute for College Access & Success. (2019). *Quick facts about student debt.* ticas.org/files/pub_files/qf_about_student_debt.pdf

Institute of International Education. (2017, October 2). *IIE study shows that studying abroad has a direct impact on skills needed for career success.* www.iie.org/employability

Interfaith Youth Core. (2019, September 30). *Friendships matter: The role of peer relationships in interfaith learning and development.* www.ifyc.org/resources/friendships-matter-role-peer-relationships-interfaith-learning-and-development

Johns, M. (2018, May 10). *Architecture students build outdoor gathering space for community bike shop.* Tulane University. https://news.tulane.edu/news/architecture-students-build-outdoor-gathering-space-community-bike-shop

Johnston, A. (2019, June 14). One surprising barrier to college success: Dense higher education lingo. *Hechinger Report.* hechingerreport.org/one-surprising-barrier-to-success-in-college-understanding-higher-education-lingo/

Kezar, A. (2018). *How colleges change: Understanding, learning, and enacting change* (2nd ed.). Routledge.

Kirp, D. L. (2019a). How university presidents can make equity and student success their top priority. Association of Public and Land Grant Universities. aplu.org/news-and-media/blog/how-university-presidents-can-make-equity-and-student-success-their-top-priority

Kirp, D. L. (2019b). *The college dropout scandal.* Oxford University Press.

Klopfenstein, K. (2019, August 08). CARE jumpstarts first-generation students' college journey. *Florida State University News.* news.fsu.edu/news/2019/08/08/care-jumpstarts-first-generation-students-college-journey/

Klunder, J. (2019, June 10). College admissions scandal reminds students to seek the best fit for their educations. *Los Angeles Times*. https://www. latimes.com/socal/daily-pilot/opinion/tn-dpt-me-college-admissions-scandal-sage-commentary-20190610-story.html

Köber, C., & Habermas, T. (2017). Parents' traces in life: When and how parents are presented in spontaneous life narratives. *Journal of Personality*, *86*(4), 679–697. doi.org/10.1111/jopy.12350

Kremer, M., & Levy, D. (2008). Peer effects and alcohol use among college students. *Journal of Economic Perspectives*, *22*(3), 189–206. doi.org/10.1257/jep.22.3.189

Kuh, G. D. (2008). *High-impact educational practices: What they are, who has access to them, and why they matter*. Association of American Colleges and Universities.

Kuh, G., O'Donnell, K., & Schneider, C. G. (2017). HIPs at ten. *Change: The Magazine of Higher Learning*, *49*(5), 8–16. doi.org/10.1080/00091383.2017.1366805

Kyte, S. B., (2017). *Who does work work for?* ACT Center for Equity in Learning. equityinlearning.act.org/wp-content/uploads/2017/08/WhoDoesWork-WorkFor.pdf

Lambert, L. M., Husser, J., & Felten, P. (2018, August 22). Mentors play critical role in quality of college experience, new poll suggests. *The Conversation*. theconversation.com/mentors-play-critical-role-in-quality-of-college-experience-new-poll-suggests-101861

Leonhardt, D., & Chinoy, S. (2019, May 23). The college dropout crisis. *The New York Times*. www.nytimes.com/interactive/2019/05/23/opinion/sunday/college-graduation-rates-ranking.html

Liu, C. H., Stevens, C., Wong, S. H., Yasui, M., & Chen, J. A. (2018). The prevalence and predictors of mental health diagnoses and suicide among U.S. college students: Implications for addressing disparities in service use. *Depression and Anxiety*, *36*(1), 8–17. doi.org/10.1002/da.22830

Long, B. T. (2008). *What is known about the impact of financial aid? Implications for policy* (Working Paper). National Center for Postsecondary Research. eric.ed.gov/?id=ED501555

Love, H., May, R. W., Cui, M., & Fincham, F. D. (2019). Helicopter parenting, self-control, and school burnout among emerging adults. *Journal of Child and Family Studies*, *29*, 327–337. doi.org/10.1007/s10826-019-01560-z

Ma, J., Pender, M., & Welch, M. (2019). *Education pays 2019: The benefits of higher education for individuals and society*. College Board. research.college-board.org/pdf/education-pays-2019-full-report.pdf

Maddux, W. W., & Galinsky, A. D. (2009). Cultural borders and mental barriers: The relationship between living abroad and creativity. *Journal of Personality and Social Psychology*, *96*(5), 1047–1061. doi.org/10.1037/a0014861

Maietta, H. (2016, November 01). *Career development needs of first-generation students*. National Association of Colleges and Employers. www.naceweb.org/career-development/special-populations/career-development-needs-of-first-generation-students/

Martin, C. C. (2019). High socioeconomic status predicts substance use and alcohol consumption in U.S. undergraduates. *Substance Use & Misuse*, *54*(6), 1035–1043. doi.org/10.1080/10826084.2018.1559193

Marx, B. M., & Turner, L. J. (2019). Student loan nudges: Experimental evidence on borrowing and educational attainment. *American Economic Journal: Economic Policy, 11*(2), 108–141. doi.org/10.1257/pol.20180279

Marx, D. M., & Goff, P. A. (2005). Clearing the air: The effect of experimenter race on target's test performance and subjective experience. *British Journal of Social Psychology, 44*(4), 645–657. doi.org/10.1348/014466604x17948

Mayhew, M. J., Rockenbach, A. B., Bowman, N. A., Seifert, T. A., & Wolniak, G. C. (2016). *How college affects students: 21st century evidence that higher education works*. Jossey-Bass.

McFarland, J., Hussar, B., Zhang, J., Wang, X., Wang, K., Hein, S., Diliberti, M., Forrest Cataldi, E., Bullock Mann, F., and Barmer, A. (2019). *The condition of education 2019* (NCES 2019-144). National Center for Education Statistics, U.S. Department of Education. nces.ed.gov/pubsearch/pubsinfo.asp?pubid=2019144

McMurtrie, B. (2018, May 25). Georgia State U. made its graduation rate jump. How? *Chronicle of Higher Education*. www.chronicle.com/article/Georgia-State-U-Made-Its/243514

Mehta, N., Stinebrickner, R., & Stinebrickner, T. (2018). Time-use and academic peer effects in college. *Economic Inquiry, 57*(1), 162–171. doi.org/10.1111/ecin.12730

Miller, A. L., Rocconi, L. M., & Dumford, A. D. (2017). Focus on the finish line: Does high-impact practice participation influence career plans and early job attainment? *Higher Education, 75*(3), 489–506. doi.org/10.1007/s10734-017-0151-z

Min, S., & Taylor, M. G. (2018). Racial and ethnic variation in the relationship between student loan debt and the transition to first birth. *Demography, 55*(1), 165–188. doi.org/10.1007/s13524-017-0643-6

Moody, J. (2019, August 28). Staying on track: A guide to academic advising. *U.S. News & World Report*. https://www.usnews.com/education/best-colleges/articles/2019-08-28/staying-on-track-a-guide-to-academic-advising

Morse, R. (2019, August 15). Debunking myths about *U.S. News* best colleges [Blog post]. *U.S. News & World Report*. www.usnews.com/education/blogs/college-rankings-blog/articles/2019-08-15/debunking-myths-about-us-news-best-colleges

Mumford, K. (2020, February 01). Student selection into an income-share agreement. Purdue University. krannert.purdue.edu/faculty/kjmumfor/papers/Mumford%20Income%20Share%20Agreement%20Selection.pdf

Nadworny, E. (Reporter); (2019, October 2). Uncovering a huge mystery of college: Office hours. In *All Things Considered*. National Public Radio. www.npr.org/2019/10/02/766568824/uncovering-a-huge-mystery-of-college-office-hours

National Association of Colleges and Employers. (2016, March 23). *Paid interns/co-ops see greater offer rates and salary offers than their unpaid classmates*. https://www.naceweb.org/job-market/internships/paid-interns-co-ops-see-greater-offer-rates-and-salary-offers-than-their-unpaid-classmates/

National Association of Colleges and Employers. (2018, May 01). *2018 internship & co-op survey report*. https://www.naceweb.org/uploadedfiles/files/2018/publication/executive-summary/2018-nace-internship-and-co-op-survey-executive-summary.pdf

National Association of Colleges and Employers. (n.d.). *Career readiness defined*. www.naceweb.org/career-readiness/competencies/career-readiness-defined/

National Center for Education Statistics. (2017a). Digest of education statistics 2017, Table 311.15. U.S. Department of Education. nces.ed.gov/programs/digest/d17/tables/dt17_311.15.asp

National Center for Education Statistics. (2017b). *Beginning college students who change their majors within 3 years of enrollment* (Publication No. 2018-434). U.S. Department of Education. nces.ed.gov/pubs2018/2018434.pdf

National Student Clearinghouse Research Center. (2019a, September 26). *Tracking transfer*. nscresearchcenter.org/signaturereport13/

National Student Clearinghouse Research Center. (2019b, December 5). *Persistence & retention—2019*. nscresearchcenter.org/snapshotreport35-first-year-persistence-and-retention/

Nilson, L. B. (2016). *Teaching at its best: A research-based resource for college instructors*. Jossey-Bass.

Nova, A. (2019, May 31). To get a bigger paycheck after college, start working now. *CNBC*. www.cnbc.com/2019/05/31/college-students-who-hold-a-job-end-up-with-higher-paychecks-later-on.html

Nussbaum, M. C. (1998). *Cultivating humanity: A classical defense of reform in liberal education*. Harvard University Press.

Oreopoulos, P., & Salvanes, K. G. (2011). Priceless: The nonpecuniary benefits of schooling. *Journal of Economic Perspectives, 25*(1), 159–184. doi.org/10.1257/jep.25.1.159

O'Shea, J. (2014). *Gap year: How delaying college changes people in ways the world needs*. John Hopkins University Press.

Padgett, R. D., Johnson, M. P., & Pascarella, E. T. (2012). First-generation undergraduate students and the impacts of the first year of college: Additional evidence. *Journal of College Student Development, 53*(2), 243–266. doi.org/10.1353/csd.2012.0032

Page, L. C., & Scott-Clayton, J. (2016). Improving college access in the United

States: Barriers and policy responses. *Economics of Education Review, 51,* 4–22. doi.org/10.1016/j.econedurev.2016.02.009

Pascarella, E. T., & Terenzini, P. T. (2005). *How college affects students.* Jossey-Bass.

Pascarella, E. T., Whitt, F. J., Edison, M. I., Nora, A., Hagedorn, L. S., Yeager, P. M., & Terenzini, P. T. (1997). Women's perceptions of a "chilly climate" and their cognitive outcomes during the first year of college. *Journal of College Student Development, 38,* 109–124.

Pasquerella, L. (2019, September 19). Yes, employers do value liberal arts degrees. *Harvard Business Review.* hbr.org/2019/09/yes-employers-do-value-liberal-arts-degrees

Patrick, B. C., Hisley, J., & Kempler, T. (2000). "What's everybody so excited about?": The effects of teacher enthusiasm on student intrinsic motivation and vitality. *Journal of Experimental Education, 68*(3), 217–236. doi.org/10.1080/00220970009600093

Potter, S., Howard, R., Murphy, S., & Moynihan, M. M. (2018). Long-term impacts of college sexual assaults on women survivors' educational and career attainments. *Journal of American College Health, 66*(6), 496–507. doi.org/10.1080/07448481.2018.1440574

Princeton University. (n.d.). *The senior thesis.* https://admission.princeton.edu/academics/senior-thesis

Protopsaltis, S., & Baum, S. (2019). Does online education live up to its promise? A look at the evidence and implications for federal policy. mason.gmu.edu/~sprotops/OnlineEd.pdf

Pryor, J. H., Eagan, K., Palucki Blake, L., Hurtado, S., Berdan, J., & Case, M. H. (2012). *The American freshman: National norms fall 2012.* Higher Education Research Institute.

Reason, R. D., Terenzini, P. T., & Domingo, R. J. (2006). First things first: Developing academic competence in the first year of college. *Research in Higher Education, 47*(2), 149–175. doi.org/10.1007/s11162-005-8884-4

Reaves, B. A. (2015). *Campus law enforcement, 2011–12.* (NCJ 248-028). Office of Justice Programs, U.S. Department of Justice. www.bjs.gov/content/pub/pdf/cle1112.pdf

Resilience Project. (2018, August 1). FSU student resilience project: About this site. https://strong.fsu.edu/wp-content/uploads/2018/08/About-project.pdf

Riegle-Crumb, C., King, B., & Irizarry, Y. (2019). Does STEM stand out? Examining racial/ethnic gaps in persistence across postsecondary fields. *Educational Researcher, 48*(3), 133–144. doi.org/10.3102/0013189x19831006

Robbins, A. (2019, March 12). Kids are the victims of the elite-college obsession. *The Atlantic.* https://www.theatlantic.com/ideas/archive/2019/03/college-bribe-scandal-shows-elite-college-obsession/584719/

Roksa, J., & Kinsley, P. (2018). The role of family support in facilitating academic success of low-income students. *Research in Higher Education, 60*(4), 415–436. doi.org/10.1007/s11162-018-9517-z

Schiffrin, H. H., Liss, M., Miles-McLean, H., Geary, K. A., Erchull, M. J., & Tashner, T. (2013). Helping or hovering? The effects of helicopter parenting on college students' well-being. *Journal of Child and Family Studies, 23*(3), 548–557. doi.org/10.1007/s10826-013-9716-3

Schulze, E., & Tomal, A. (2006). The chilly classroom: Beyond gender. *College Teaching, 54*(3), 263–270. doi.org/10.3200/ctch.54.3.263-270

Scott-Clayton, J., & Minaya, V. (2016). Should student employment be subsidized? Conditional counterfactuals and the outcomes of work-study participation. *Economics of Education Review, 52*, 1–18. doi.org/10.1016/j.econedurev.2015.06.006

Sellami, N., Shaked, S., Laski, F. A., Eagan, K. M., & Sanders, E. R. (2017). Implementation of a learning assistant program improves student performance on higher-order assessments. *CBE Life Sciences Education, 16*(4), ar62. doi.org/10.1187/cbe.16-12-0341

Shapiro, D., Ryu, M., Huie, F., & Liu, Q. (2019, October 30). *Some college, no degree: A 2019 snapshot for the nation and 50 states.* National Student Clearinghouse Research Center. nscresearchcenter.org/some-college-no-degree-2019/

Sigelman, M., Taska, B., Restuccia, D., Braganza, S., & Bittle, S. (2018, October). *Majors that matter: Ensuring college graduates avoid underemployment.* Burning Glass Technologies. www.burning-glass.com/wp-content/uploads/underemployment_majors_that_matter_final.pdf

Sinozich, S., & Langton, L. (2014). Rape and sexual assault victimization among college-age females, 1995–2013. (NCJ 248-471). Office of Justice Programs, U.S. Department of Justice. www.bjs.gov/content/pub/pdf/rsavcaf9513.pdf

Smith, B. L. (2004). *Learning communities: Reforming undergraduate education.* John Wiley & Sons.

Stephens, N. M., Hamedani, M. G., & Destin, M. (2014). Closing the social-class achievement gap. *Psychological Science, 25*(4), 943–953. doi.org/10.1177/0956797613518349

Strada-Gallup. (2018). *Strada-Gallup alumni survey: Mentoring college students to success.* https://news.gallup.com/reports/244031/2018-strada-gallup-alumni-survey-mentoring-students.aspx

Strayhorn, T. L. (2018). *College students' sense of belonging: A key to educational success for all students.* Routledge. doi.org/10.4324/9781315297293

Strumbos, D., Linderman, D., & Hicks, C. C. (2018). Postsecondary pathways out of poverty: City University of New York Accelerated Study in Associate Programs and the case for national policy. *RSF: The Russell Sage Foundation Journal of the Social Sciences, 4*(3), 100–117. doi.org/10.7758/rsf.2018.4.3.06

Struthers, C. W., Perry, R. P., & Menec, V. H. (2000). An examination of the relationship among academic stress, coping, motivation, and performance in college. *Research in Higher Education, 41*(5), 581–592. doi:10.1023/a:1007094931292

Supiano, B. (2018, May 06). Traditional teaching may deepen inequality. Can a different approach fix it? *Chronicle of Higher Education*. www.chronicle.com/article/Traditional-Teaching-May/243339

Sutton, H. (2019). Research shows 'new epidemic' of students with anxiety. *Disability Compliance for Higher Education, 24*(11), 9. doi.org/10.1002/dhe.30654

Theobald, E. J., Hill, M. J., Tran, E., Agrawal, S., Arroyo, E. N., Behling, S., Chambwe, N., Laboy Cintrón, D., Cooper, J. D., Dunster, G., Grummer, J. A., Hennessey, K., Hsiao, J., Iranon, N., Jones, L., Jordt, H, Keller, M., Lacey, M. E., Littlefield, A. L., . . . Freeman, S. (2020, March 24). Active learning narrows achievement gaps for underrepresented students in undergraduate science, technology, engineering, and math. *Proceedings of the National Academy of Sciences, 117*(12), 6476–6483. doi.org/10.1073/pnas.1916903117

Thielking, M. (2017, February 06). A dangerous wait: Colleges can't meet soaring student needs for mental health care. National Alliance on Mental Illness. https://namiswwa.org/dangerous-wait-colleges-cant-meet-soaring-student-needs-mental-health-care/

Tough, P. (2014, May 15). Who gets to graduate? *The New York Times Magazine*. www.nytimes.com/2014/05/18/magazine/who-gets-to-graduate.html

Tulane University. (n.d.). *Committed to community*. https://tulane.edu/life-tulane/committed-community

U.S. Department of Education. (2015, July 27). *Fact sheet: Focusing higher education on student success*. www.ed.gov/news/press-releases/fact-sheet-focusing-higher-education-student-success

U.S. Department of Education. (2019, September 25). *National federal student loan cohort default rate continues to decline*. www.ed.gov/news/press-releases/national-federal-student-loan-cohort-default-rate-continues-decline

U.S. News & World Report. (2020). *2020: Most students in sororities*. www.usnews.com/best-colleges/rankings/most-sororities

University Interfaith Council. (n.d.). *University Interfaith Council at University of California, Santa Cruz*. http://www.ucscuic.org/

University of California–Riverside. (n.d.). *Service*. https://studentlife.ucr.edu/service

University of California–San Diego. (n.d.). *UC San Diego competencies*. Engaged Learning Tools UC San Diego. elt.ucsd.edu/competencies/index.html

University of Cincinnati. (n.d.). *Capstone experience*. College of Arts & Sciences, University of Cincinnati. www.artsci.uc.edu/departments/biology/undergrad/capstone.html

University of Connecticut (n.d.) *Annual career fairs and events*. https://career. uconn.edu/resources/category/annual-career-fairs-events/

University of Delaware Police Department. (n.d.). *Accreditation*. www1.udel. edu/police/about-us/accreditation.html

University of Kentucky. (n.d.). *Academic initiatives for students*. www.uky.edu/ housing/initiatives-housed-residence-life

University of Michigan. (n.d.). *Undergraduate Research Opportunity Program: About us*. lsa.umich.edu/urop/about-us.html

University of Nebraska–Omaha. (n.d.). *Fall 2019 Service Learning Academy newsletter*. issuu.com/unosla-unomaha/docs/fall_2019_newsletter

University of Oregon. (n.d.). *Sexual violence prevention*. Dean of Students. dos. uoregon.edu/svpe

University of Texas at Austin. (n.d.). *360 connections*. Undergraduate Studies, University of Texas. ugs.utexas.edu/360

University of Vermont. (n.d.). *Wellness environment*. https://www.uvm.edu/we

Upcraft, M. L., Gardner, J. N., & Barefoot, B. O. (2005). *Challenging and supporting the first-year student: A handbook for improving the first year of college*. Jossey-Bass.

Vandal, B. (2019, January 24). *Why momentum pathways?* Complete College America. completecollege.org/article/why-momentum-pathways/

Vasold, K. L., Kosowski, L. E., & Pivarnik, J. M. (2019). Academic success and 1 year of intramural sports participation by freshmen students. *Journal of College Student Retention: Research, Theory & Practice*. doi. org/10.1177/1521025119833000

Venit, E. (2016, August 29). *How late is too late?* EAB. eab.com/technology/ whitepaper/student-success/how-late-is-too-late/

Venit, E. (2017, August 21). *Why even C students should consider taking 15 credits their first semester*. EAB. eab.com/insights/blogs/student-success/ why-even-c-students-should-consider-taking-15-credits-their-first-semester/

Venit, E., & Bevevino, D. (2020). *The student success playbook*. EAB. attachment.eab.com/wp-content/uploads/2020/02/PDF-Navigate-Student-Success-Playbook-Feb2020.pdf

Wellock, B. (2019, November 13). FSU research: Helicopter parenting hinders children's self-control skills. *Florida State University News*. news. fsu.edu/news/2019/11/13/fsu-research-helicopter-parenting-hinders-childrens-self-control-skills

Woolf, T. (2019). Navigating college life. *University of South Florida Magazine*. www.usf.edu/magazine/2019-fall/

Woolfenden, S., & Stevenson, B. (2011). *Establishing appropriate staffing levels for campus public safety departments*. Office of Community Oriented Policing Services, U.S. Department of Justice. cops.usdoj.gov/RIC/Publications/ cops-p210-pub.pdf

Wyner, G. (2019, November 11). "Illuminate Tech" speaker series to fea-
    ture students. Georgia Tech News Center. news.gatech.edu/2019/11/06/
    illuminate-tech-speaker-series-feature-students

Yi, A. (2016, July 29). *Why texting your students isn't "coddling."* EAB. https://
    eab.com/insights/blogs/student-success/why-texting-your-students-isnt-
    coddling/

Young, J. R. (2019, August 30). Explaining the value of the liberal arts. *Ed-
    Surge.* www.edsurge.com/news/2019-08-28-explaining-the-value-of-the-
    liberal-arts

Index

About the Author

Joe O'Shea is dean of Undergraduate Studies and assistant provost at Florida State University, where he helps lead the university's nationally recognized student success initiatives. Joe also serves as a higher education expert for the U.S. Department of Education and other national efforts. A Truman and Rhodes Scholar, Joe has a master's degree in comparative social policy and a PhD in education from the University of Oxford. He is the author of the book *Gap Year: How Delaying College Changes People in Ways the World Needs*.